Ethel

The biography
of countryside pioneer
Ethel Haythornthwaite

Ethel

Helen Mort

Vertebrate Publishing, Sheffield
www.adventurebooks.com

Ethel
Helen Mort

First published in 2024 by Vertebrate Publishing.

 VERTEBRATE PUBLISHING
Omega Court, 352 Cemetery Road, Sheffield S11 8FT, United Kingdom.
www.adventurebooks.com

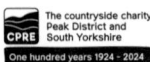 Published in partnership with
CPRE Peak District and South Yorkshire.
www.cprepdsy.org.uk

This biography was made possible by a generous legacy to CPRE Peak District and South Yorkshire from the estate of the late David Wilson – a supporter of the charity for over seventy years.

Copyright © Helen Mort 2024.
Foreword copyright © Fiona Reynolds 2024.

The Pride of the Peak by Ethel Bassett Gallimore was first published in 1926 by Jonathan Cape. It is reproduced here by permission of the trustees of CPRE Peak District and South Yorkshire, on behalf of the Haythornthwaite estate.

Extracts from *Thinking with Trees* by Jason Allen-Paisant (© Jason Allen-Paisant 2021, published by Carcanet Press) and *The Poems of Norman MacCaig* by Norman MacCaig (© the estate of Norman MacCaig 2009, published by Polygon, an imprint of Birlinn Ltd) are reproduced with permission of the Licensors through PLSclear.

Front cover: Ethel in her beloved Peak District.
Back cover: Ethel addressing a 1930s Ramblers' rally for access in Winnats Pass.
Photography and images © CPRE PDSY unless otherwise credited. All of the photographs credited to CPRE PDSY were sourced from their archives; in most cases the photographer cannot be readily identified.

Helen Mort has asserted her rights under the Copyright, Designs and Patents Act 1988 to be identified as author of this work.

This book is a work of non-fiction. The author has stated to the publishers that, except in such minor respects not affecting the substantial accuracy of the work, the contents of the book are true.

A CIP catalogue record for this book is available from the British Library.

ISBN: 978-1-83981-229-3 (Paperback)
ISBN: 978-1-83981-230-9 (Ebook)

10 9 8 7 6 5 4 3 2 1

All rights reserved. No part of this work covered by the copyright herein may be reproduced or used in any form or by any means – graphic, electronic, or mechanised, including photocopying, recording, taping or information storage and retrieval systems – without the written permission of the publisher.

Every effort has been made to obtain the necessary permissions with reference to copyright material, both illustrative and quoted. We apologise for any omissions in this respect and will be pleased to make the appropriate acknowledgements in any future edition.

Vertebrate Publishing is committed to printing on paper from sustainable sources.

Printed and bound in the UK by TJ Books Limited, Padstow, Cornwall.

Contents

I *Ethel*	vii
Foreword by Dame Fiona Reynolds	xi
Prologue	1
An Opening	5
Endcliffe Vale	15
Aching Delight	27
Longshaw and Blacka Moor	37
The Threat to the Peak	51
Vast Architecture	61
The Belt	75
A National Park	87
Peace and Amber Light	103
Key Sources and Further Reading	109
Acknowledgements	111
II *The Pride of the Peak* by Ethel Bassett Gallimore	113

I
Ethel

Foreword

There are tensions running cleverly, intriguingly, throughout this book. Tensions that evoke the gritty reality, complexity and sheer effort of the conservation task; a task that never stands still. In this frank, open and generous biography, Helen Mort gives us new insights into Ethel Haythornthwaite's remarkable life and work and poses some piercing questions for those inheriting her mantle.

First, there's Ethel herself. Born into wealth but possessing a deep sense of public purpose, thrift and unwavering commitment, she was a wondrous, spirited young woman who, widowed at twenty-two, found a redemptive mission in saving the countryside from the horrors of thoughtless suburbanisation. Not for Ethel loud protests: she was a letter writer, not a street fighter. But she was effective. First in stopping litter, then persuading city leaders not to allow houses to be built on Sheffield's beautiful fringes, then buying land (as at Longshaw, which she gave to the National Trust) to safeguard it forever. What she achieved was done through love: of place and of beauty, but also done *with* love. Having lost her beloved husband Henry Gallimore in the First World War tragically soon after their marriage, she threw herself into protecting the places that meant so much to her. Twenty years later she found her new helpmeet: architect and fellow campaigner Gerald Haythornthwaite, whom she married and with whom she thereafter fought her cause.

Then there are the tensions between Sheffield, the dark, industry-stained city, and Ethel's beloved Peak District: sometimes wild, sometimes friendly; always moody and glorious; and beautifully evoked here by Helen Mort. It's an inspiring landscape that refuses to be categorised, that is always changing yet exemplifies the continuity we yearn for. The turmoil of urban Sheffield versus the calm, aesthetic beauty of the Peak District runs like a continuous stream throughout this narrative, posing a burning set of contrasts, though Ethel forces us to connect them. Above all it raises questions

... what, in fact, is conservation? For whom and why do we care about beauty? Does beauty matter if there is no one left to enjoy it? Ethel's cause required the separation of town from country, to stop sprawl and protect the countryside, and her far-sighted campaign for the Sheffield green belt exemplifies her success. Today, it's clear we need the green belt more than ever, though it needs to work harder and achieve more in itself in the face of continuing pressures.

And third, the future. Ethel's cause was primarily and uncompromisingly aesthetic, stopping bad things from happening and persuading, through design guides and education, better standards among architects and builders. But today we know about deeper problems: the catastrophic decline in nature and public health, and the looming crisis of climate change. So, what lies ahead for Ethel's legacy and the continuing task of conservation when people's priorities seem ever more short-term, yet the long-term need for more sustainable solutions is ever more urgent? Once again, we find that she has laid the best possible foundations. The Peak District National Park for which she fought so hard now has a bigger role to play than she could possibly have imagined, as we look to our protected landscapes to find answers to complex interrelated problems like how to live and manage land sustainably, enable nature to recover, and enhance people's mental and physical well-being.

For organisations like CPRE who continue Ethel's 'genteel' fight, the judgemental language she and Gerald used to criticise poor development (*vulgar, shoddy, deplorable*) is no longer appropriate or acceptable. And we've certainly moved on from concerns about aesthetics to recognising a deeper definition of beauty as sustainability within a broader environmental framework. But in a world driven by instant gratification and materialism, I long for the clarity of Ethel's principled, clear and far-sighted approach. Notwithstanding her many successes, I think she'd be pretty horrified by the short distance we have travelled as a society in embracing her high and unremitting standards.

This warm, affectionate biography strikes a new note. Not reverence, not blind admiration, but curiosity explored, humanity contemplated, and all underpinned by love. A love shared between the author and Ethel for the beauty of the countryside around Sheffield but which now needs expanding to embrace an even deeper love for Sheffield itself, wherein we now know lie the solutions as well as many of the problems.

These people – Ethel and her many allies, some conscious, some

FOREWORD

unconscious – have made it possible for us to face the future with more confidence. We stand on her slender shoulders and derive strength from her ideals, but we must exert our own courage and imagination to respond to the greater challenges we face today. I salute Helen Mort for her original, honest and remarkable story of a woman whose legacy enables us all to seek a better future.

Dame Fiona Reynolds
Coates, Gloucestershire
December 2023

Ethel

What is this life that's stirring in my veins?

Just Stanage. Evening. What remains
is sky with the light burned out of it,
or rock with our touch gone from it.

Listen: a half-remembered story,
rooted like heather in the memory,
words said by the dead to the living,
repeated by the living to the dead.

(the wind through grass sounds like
instead instead instead instead)

What is this life...?

If I find out, Ethel, I'll let you know.
My guesses move the way a paraglider
sews currents of air above Mam Tor.
Your voice. My voice. Nothing more

(the wind above the nothing, sweetest
nothing of the moors)

'… only earth's high beauties held me sane.'

Ethel Bassett Gallimore, 1926

Ethel, later in life, walking into Ecclesall Woods, part of the green belt she helped to create.

Prologue

What is this life that's stirring in my veins?
The fire of morn, the ferth to roam outdoors.
Nothing can hold me, nought my freedom reins,
I am mounting like a bird unto the moors …
    (from *The Pride of the Peak* by Ethel Bassett Gallimore)

These words are climbing words. They are written to a heartbeat, the breath and footsteps of a young woman with winter-bark-coloured hair and sturdy boots. She goes lightly from rock to rock, sometimes almost skipping. We are watching her from a distance. We might not exist without her.

She is not alone: her sister Gertie is nearby, the chauffeur waiting in the family car back on the road. But she is making a path towards the lip of Stanage with her body. Leaning into the wind, she is italicised. All of her is a question: *what is this life? What is this life? What is this life?* She is unmoored in hers, a widow at the age of twenty-two. Grief has whittled her thin. But out here on the moor, even in harsh weather, she is grounded, a sapling with its roots in the earth. She puts one foot in front of the other. Her body is writing new sentences. All she must do is find the next word. Her name is Ethel. She is making her steady progress through the world.

Sheffield, summer 2023

Dear Guardian of the Peak –

Dear Ethel –

Dear Mrs Haythornthwaite –

You were a woman who understood the power of a letter: one heart to another, transmitted on paper. Something that could be held in the hand, the ink traced, the places where the pen left its grooves still visible. Letters come from the body, not just from the mind. You wrote them religiously, you answered them faithfully.

You wrote to persuade and to preserve, but you also wrote to tell people that they were held in your mind. It is there in the letters you received, watermarked with each kindness. From your niece, saying, 'thank you very much for the coat hangers, they are very, very beautiful and I am always short at school'. From Luisa, who wrote, 'thank you for the calendar with the fine view of the Langdale Pikes. We actually saw them from Lingmoor and also from the summit of Bow Fell ... How many lovely valleys owe their very existence to your gallant Fight For Beauty?' And it is there in a letter from the Lord Mayor of Sheffield, thanking you on behalf of the townspeople for your tireless work.

Summer in Sheffield, decades after your death. What am I supposed to do with these complicated riches? Hay fever and your legacy. A deadline, an empty screen and somebody butchering a tree streets away with a chainsaw, the air protesting loudly. I'm surrounded by paper. Minutes from your meetings. Posters and poetry. Summer drought, dry eyes, the grass on the suburban lawns bleaching outside.

I'm no biographer. But I am obsessed with the story of your life. I don't believe in nothing-but-the-truth, but I do believe in the whole truth, and that's something different. The whole truth is my feet under the desk, blistered from running skylines you knew like the ridges of your own knuckles. It's my tabby cat, leaping down from the shed roof and landing awkwardly, righting itself with its tail, lemur-like – that way cats have of styling every movement out, making it seem intentional. Writing is like that. I think you know: your poetry is earnest and haunting, and its veins are full of place names, route maps, a litany of Derbyshire hills. I love that. I love how you are not afraid of unbridled praise; sometimes I think it isn't fashionable now.

The whole truth is that, as I type this, fires have been raging across Burbage Moor. The photographs were apocalyptic. Bloody skies, blackened ground. The truth is that much of what I can see if I run uphill from my house and don't stop until I'm at the edge of Houndkirk or Stanage is as wild and valued and exhilarating as it ever was, but the planet it lodges on, the planet I lodge on, is ailing, and we're all stupefied by complicity. I'm glad you didn't live to see that.

The whole truth is that we talk about 'unspoiled' places as if they exist, as if it's possible for us to be near them and not ruin them with our own needs. The truth is that even this way of writing is part of the problem, positioning us all as separate, distanced. The truth, I think, is that you always put yourself second, thought yourself less valuable than the Peak District. The truth is that nobody really knows how to do that any more; we wouldn't know even if our lives depended on it. And they do.

You wrote so many letters. You wrote to people, and you wrote to the landscape you loved. All your life, you addressed yourself to the Peak District. It only seems fair that we should write back to you now.

Yours faithfully –
Yours thankfully –
Yours for now –
Helen

Ethel in the grounds of Endcliffe Vale House, most likely in the war years.

An Opening

Come climb, come wander, come and view a thing
More vast, unclenchable than aught before ...
(The Pride of the Peak)

Ethel Haythornthwaite was a pioneer: an activist, a leader and a poet. But you can walk around her home town asking people if they've heard of her and be greeted by puzzled silence. 'Ethel who?'

We begin in the landscape Ethel grew up in: the centre of England, on the gritstone lip of Sheffield, home to over 580,000 people and countless more stories. It is a city whose place in the public imagination has been shaped by steelworks, by buffer girls, by cutlery and by *The Full Monty*; known for its proximity to moors and rock-climbing destinations, hills and dales, neat villages, the extraordinary variety of neighbouring Derbyshire. A green city, a city of direct action, fights to defend street trees. Half the preserve of Arctic Monkeys' first album and half the wildness fought for in the Kinder mass trespass of 1932.

'My God, how does one write a Biography?' Virginia Woolf once asked, words that would haunt those who tried, like her acclaimed biographer Hermione Lee. How does anyone begin? Is it audacious to even try? If this is to be an account of Ethel Haythornthwaite, it is also an account of the Peak District, the landscape she saw herself utterly entwined with. Then where does the Peak District begin? Addressing each question only reveals another. In *The Threat to the Peak*, published in 1931, Ethel would write:

> It is perhaps best to approach the Peak District from the south. We can thus observe, as we traverse it to its northern limit, the increasing wildness of the landscape. Nature gradually reasserts herself and man's dominance declines until we reach the high moors where she is still in undisputed possession, and where the struggle for life is waged on a scene and greater scale and among elemental conditions

of greater intensity than those that prevail in the warmer and more sheltered parts.

There is a sense here of the Derbyshire landscape intensifying, growing into itself almost. As a child in Chesterfield, I would have first approached that landscape from the south-east side of what is now the national park, noticing how the undulations became rocky waves. The journey north-west across to the Snake Pass when we travelled to my grandparents' house in Oldham certainly felt imbued with a sense of growing drama, from sheep-grazed fields to misty tops beyond the reservoir at Ladybower. I always longed to get out of the car and run into the ominous, hammered-silver sky.

As an adult, as someone who has written about Derbyshire obsessively in fiction and poetry, who has climbed and walked and run marathons across the breadth of it, I no longer see the Peak District as something which 'begins'. If I try to think of it, I see the road between grit-encircled Hathersage and Sheffield. As you leave the Hope Valley and the road flattens near Surprise View, there's a *Welcome to Sheffield* sign. Soon after, another that says, *Welcome to Derbyshire*. A little further down the road and you pass *Welcome to Sheffield* again. You are weaving in and out of a defined landscape, one whose definition has acquired almost sacred significance, passing through these hallowed borders in an almost nonchalant way.

John Ruskin's famous caricature of Sheffield city as 'a dirty picture in a golden frame' is a beguiling one, but it no longer rings true either, however apt it may have been in South Yorkshire's industrial heyday. My objection is not just to the 'dirty picture' (Sheffield in 2024 is a map of green space as well as a hive of industries). This 'frame' is not golden and fixed. It is the spreading bruise of purple autumn heather and the mottled greys of wet limestone. It is light touching the early morning water at Redmires; how the whole scene changes in an instant, from thick mist to sudden, clarifying sun. It might 'surround' Sheffield, but it is permeable. The city and the moors bleed into one another, mixed watercolours. There is a constant exchange between them, osmosis. The city returns the glance of the countryside and vice versa. They are porous. It is a dynamic which requires compassion, responsibility and a degree of regulation – an understanding that urban and rural spaces influence each other.

The extraordinary life of Ethel Haythornthwaite is emblematic of that complex porosity. She drew on an industrial family fortune and the social networks of the city to protect and preserve the 'wild' places of Derbyshire.

The 'dirty picture' reinforcing the 'golden frame'. In turn, she was partially motivated by wanting to maintain the rich natural resources and unique spaces of the Peak District for city people, for the returning heroes of the Second World War. In a sense, there was no separation. The binary of rural and urban can be unhelpful. Our fates are intertwined: an idea which is returning to popular discourse as we contemplate the bleak effects of our current climate emergency.

This book is not a straight line. Its edges are permeable too. It is an account of one restless woman looking for another, in the imprints under Burbage Edge, in the flow of the river at Froggatt, under the thin veil of night that falls in winter over the Longshaw Estate, when the stars make moorland frost glitter with spectral promise. It is something like the flexible boundary between the crucible of Sheffield, forged by hot metal, and the land around it. To return to Ruskin's dirty picture, it is the places where the gold rubs off on the canvas, casting it in a different light, at least for a second.

Who was Ethel Haythornthwaite and why do I owe my whole life as I know it to her? She was, as all interesting people are, myriad. She was a poet and a philanthropist, gentle and fierce, a quiet revolutionary who has been overlooked by history. She was motivated by grief and by hope. She was a Methodist who attended seances. She was an advocate and a diplomat, a sister and a friend, a woman who kept an orderly house but hated domestic work. She came from wealth, but she was frugal. She was interested in legacy, but lived for the immediacy of walking on Stanage, lines of poetry swarming in her head. She was restless and infinitely patient. Perhaps I should not think of myself as answering my question but hers: *what is this life that's stirring in my veins?*

In Matthew Kelly's book *The Women Who Saved the English Countryside*, he identifies four key figures in the protection of landscape: Sylvia Sayer, Octavia Hill, Beatrix Potter and Pauline Dower. Everything that Kelly says of his four pioneers was also true of Ethel:

> Without their work, more land would be enclosed, more land would be built on, more footpaths and access to open spaces would have been lost.

Like Ethel, 'the four were convinced that the experience of urbanisation and industrialisation alienated humanity from nature, having a terrible effect on human well-being, diminishing our capacity to even recognise our unhappiness'. As such, they 'advocated forms of environmental citizenship that identified land as public goods from which flow collective rights'.

It's here that I imagine Ethel Haythornthwaite leaning over my shoulder and muttering, 'and responsibilities. Don't forget those.' Like Ethel, they all came from privileged economic backgrounds. Like Ethel, they were all artists; this doesn't surprise me, since art connects us to the embodied self, the non-abstracted body and therefore to the land, what Nan Shepherd recognised in her prose as:

> Walking thus, hour after hour, the senses keyed, one walks the flesh transparent. But no metaphor, transparent, or light as air, is adequate. The body is not made negligible, but paramount. Flesh is not annihilated but fulfilled. One is not bodiless, but essential body.

Essential body, essential breath. Ethel was a woman who 'saved' the British countryside too. But she is difficult to categorise, difficult to capture, mysterious to us. Perhaps this makes her even more compelling. That she achieved what she achieved with a female body, subject to regulation and comment and constraint, is even more remarkable. Ethel lived between 1894 and 1986 and was doing some of her most vital work between the 1930s and 1960s. In her account of the life of poet Sylvia Plath, Heather Clark contextualises the hill that a woman with public aspirations had to climb even in the 1950s. She describes a speech given by Democratic candidate Adlai Stevenson at Plath's 1955 Smith commencement, titled 'A Purpose for Modern Woman'. The best way that female arts graduates could contribute to society, Stevenson argued, was to embrace 'the humble role of housewife, which, statistically is what most of you are going to be whether you like it or not'. Stevenson (considered a liberal in his day) went on to elaborate:

> This assignment for you as wives and mothers has great advantages. In the first place, it is home work – you can do it in the living room with a baby in your lap or a can opener in your hand. If you're really clever, maybe you can even practice your saving arts on that unsuspecting man while he's watching television.

He acknowledged that the women might feel a sense of 'lost horizons' in this vocation: 'once they wrote poetry ... now it's the laundry list ... They had hoped to play a part in the crisis of the age. But what they do is wash diapers.' He concluded archly, hoping that his view was not 'too depressing' and adding that 'women never had it so good as you do'.

This was 1955. There are many statistics, many quotes that could be used to illustrate the social position of women at the time and the expectations for their role in public life, but this one seems the starkest because it was a message delivered to new female graduates. Plath, as Clark puts it, 'took herself and her desires seriously in a world that often refused to do so'. The same could be said of Ethel Haythornthwaite, across the Atlantic. This is not to say that Ethel would have regarded herself as particularly pioneering: this is the privilege of the passage of time, the gift of overview and hindsight; we recognise her impact on our age. Ethel was a woman of remarkable foresight, her focus on preserving the future, in laying solid foundations. She was elegiac in her prose, but she was never backward-looking. Like all of us, she was mostly consumed by the day-to-day process of living, of staying alive.

In writing a spoof biography of a friend of hers, Virginia Woolf described herself as a 'bio-or-mytho-grapher'. We are all mythographers, even when the subject is ourselves: we are shrouded in stories, in claims and counterclaims. Since 'a self that goes on changing is a self that goes on living', a good biography 'is the record of things that change rather than of the things that happen'. Any life-writer must navigate the gap between the public self and the secret self. Somewhat playfully, Woolf instructed:

> Facts have their importance – but that is where the biography comes to grief. The biographer cannot extract the atom. He gives us the husk. Therefore as things are, the best method would be to separate the two kinds of truth. Let the biographer print fully, completely, accurately, the known facts without comment; Then let him write the life as fiction.

We all become somewhat fictionalised after we die. The condolence letters sent to Ethel's partner after her passing become part of her mythology. A friend observed that she was 'like Emily, in Branwell's portrait of the three Brontë sisters'. Pauline Dower, herself a national parks champion, praised her 'keen and intelligent eye' and her 'steady and unremitting work'. Sylvia Sayer, of Dartmoor fame, said that Ethel was 'an example to us all'. Cath MacKay from the Sheffield branch of the Ramblers' Association wrote: 'those who never had the pleasure of meeting her felt an acute sense of missed opportunity'. In his letter of April 1986, Maurice Kay praised her eloquence, wherein she could express any feeling to anyone so very exactly that no shadow of doubt remained … couched in such carefully chosen, benign terms that even the most out and out miscreant couldn't fail to warm to her chiding.

Perhaps the most plaintive tribute comes from a letter from Mrs Mary Moss, who simply lamented:

why don't we have more people like Ethel to bring order, beauty and love to life?

What would Ethel Haythornthwaite have thought of the notion of a book about her life and love of the Peak District? From my fleeting glimpse into her way of being in the world, I think she'd urge, 'don't write about me, write about the ever-present threats to the land'. She was willing to be in the background, doing vital legacy work that looked to the future of the organisation that would become the Sheffield branch of the Campaign to Protect Rural England. Maybe she would be standing on Devonshire Green with my teenage stepdaughter and all the other activists on the climate strike. Or perhaps she'd urge me to step away from my laptop and set off through Endcliffe Park and Bingham Park and out past Forge Dam, pass through the trees at Lady Canning's Plantation and find a remarkable stone on the exposed moorland, to contemplate its vantage point, its relationship to the things around it, the shadows it casts and the brief shadow I cast on it, human imposter, passing through and finding myself improved by the slant of things.

An early portrait of the young Ethel Ward.

Sheffield, summer 2023

Dear Ethel (if I may),

I am trying out the facts of your life. I write:

Ethel was born in Sheffield in 1894 to parents made wealthy by industry. She died in 1986. In her time, she founded the Sheffield branch of the CPRE and saved large chunks of the Peak District from development, preserving the Longshaw Estate and Blacka Moor, helping to draw up the Sheffield green belt and establishing the Peak District as the first national park in the UK. She was married first to Captain Henry Gallimore. In 1937 she married Gerald Haythornthwaite, having interviewed him for a job a year earlier. Together, they worked to shore up the future of Sheffield conservation. She had no children. She was survived by Gerald and – briefly – by her sister Gertie. She does not make the list of the most famous people in Sheffield.

All of this is true. It is such a poor summary. Then I try to be poetic. I write:

She disliked housework. She was frugal, except for her visits to Harley Street. She never bought paper clips. She seldom put on lights. At the end of her life, she had dementia. She rode a horse called Bracken and received a Rolls-Royce as a wedding present from her brother. Another brother founded a bookshop which would go on to be a branch of Waterstones. She wrote excellent poetry. She shunned direct action in favour of exerting quiet influence. Her second husband was nearly twenty years younger than her. They married quietly. She bought land herself when she had to, donated it back to the public. She wanted to fix limits on where town ended and countryside began. She always dressed for dinner. They played Handel and Bach at her funeral.

I cross it all out and vow to start again tomorrow.

I wish I could write as well as you. Your poetry is alive. It sings, louder than the rest. It gives a truer sense of the Peak District than anything I have ever read. You are excellent with colour. Green, golds, russets and olive. Maroon and bilberry turning red. Emerald moss and yellow oaks. Copper sunbeams. Stained autumn air. You rhapsodise about 'brilliant heather', how it changes our sense of the possibilities of purple, and you can never get enough of it ('on fire for more my need expands'). You also treat the landscape like a body, which I believe it is: 'let me climb up by the naked bones / Of this bold land'. You capture that sense of ancientness that we can feel, even today, in Derbyshire:

> *There is a lonely bay within the edge,*
> *High rocks it has like huge hieratic doors,*
> *A low rock in the centre of the ledge,*
> *Above the heaven, below the valley floors.*
> *Our blood is of that early brood,*
> *Uncivilized, untamed and crude:*
> *I know for all the cultured vales beneath,*
> *Here is my element and here my breath.*

Our blood is ancient and we have forgotten it. You know that this place is 'vast, unclenchable'. But you held on to what you could and you handed it on to us.

Yours –

Endcliffe Vale House. Demolished in the 1950s, it stood in the grounds of what is now the University of Sheffield's Endcliffe student village.

Endcliffe Vale

Behind the uplands green declining roll,
Before the mystic moors are stretched below.
I hasten to the hill among the hills,
Over the edge, until an open vale
Tames to a little lane, whose streamlet spills
O'er slippy stones, when warmer airs prevail …
  (*The Pride of the Peak*)

Throw a dart. Aim for the centre of England and if you're lucky you might strike Sheffield. Circled on a map of the UK, it seems a crucible, a sweet spot, a hub, just north of the country's heart. It's nestled by the eastern foothills of the Pennines, hills rising to the west, the flat, punished ground of the South Yorkshire coalfields to the east. It is contested ground: the North to some and the Midlands to others. It is Yorkshire, but only just. It is tricksy, provocative, keeping visitors on their toes. It might catch the dart and throw it back at you, its aim certainly better than yours.

Seen outlined on a map, the City of Sheffield district border looks to me like a squashed, distorted maple leaf with the stalk somewhere near Tinsley, jutting towards Rotherham, and the ragged leaves stretching out to High Green, Oughtibridge and Stocksbridge in the north, reaching to touch Burbage Moor and Houndkirk in the south-west, then Totley and Jordanthorpe, and Mosborough in the east, a stone's throw from where I grew up in the ex-coalfields of North East Derbyshire. The maple leaf has been trampled somehow, softened by rain and then moved by someone's steel-toe-capped boot.

The first map of Sheffield I ever studied was a diagram of bomb damage, hanging in the window of Rare and Racy bookshop on Devonshire Green, a den of hidden vinyls, leaning shelves, gig flyers and well-thumbed books. It made the city seem more absence than presence, more dots than lines. I pored over it, aghast. It was like staring at the prone body of a casualty, before the healing, before the long convalescence. But it makes no sense to look at Sheffield on the flat. It is a city of verticals, of seven hills and five rivers, the confluence of the Don, the Sheaf, the Rivelin, the Loxley and the Porter. Once a river-border separating the Anglo-Saxon kingdoms of Mercia and Northumbria, it is built on hillsides, the houses clinging on for dear life. It teems with trees. When I stand at the top of my street and look out at green tower blocks, the land rising to Gleadless, I feel something like dizziness. The bowl-shape of the city seems almost comforting now, each hill looking out for the others, watching benevolently. But in the wake of the Industrial Revolution, Sheffield was a dish of smog, the Don one of the most polluted rivers in Europe. When George Orwell visited, he was moved to write in *The Road to Wigan Pier* in 1937 that Sheffield 'could justly claim to be called the ugliest town in the Old World'. In the nineteenth century, the city had grown tenfold and the traces of expansion were showing, written – tattooed even – in grey and black.

'Existence in a northern industrial town can be a drab affair,' remarked Ethel, writing for *The Sheffield Schoolmaster* years later in 1962. Her piece, under the matter-of-fact title 'Living in Sheffield', conceded that the city had seen positive developments in the years since Orwell's stark verdict ('an uncommonly good repertory theatre, concerts and an art gallery of high standards'), but argued that, 'even these advantages would leave its citizens unsatisfied, those who have not lost that primal bond with the earth itself; who look up from the basin of Sheffield, climb its streams – the origins of its famous cutlery trade – and recognise how we are cradled, redeemed and blest by the surrounding hills and moors.'

The word 'blest' belies Ethel's almost religious reverence for the Peak District, and there's something of the notion of original sin in the way she describes the perils of industrial life: the 'onslaught' of motor traffic, the 'pity' she reserved for those who felt the need to dash around the country or – heaven forbid – leave it in search of greater spectacles, such as the mountains of the Alps ('it is sounder,' Ethel chided, 'to penetrate the mysteries of your own family before you wait on distant celebrities'). She branded the era she was living through 'the artificial age' and looked to gritstone and limestone for forgiveness.

'Nothing that can ever be done in Sheffield or Manchester ... can ever really give what nature, such as exists in The Peak in all its moods, can give,' she observed. I love her contemplation of landscape's moods, the mercurial sky over the Great Ridge, a sense of Derbyshire as a feeling, knowing entity, its sentiments far more profound than the brutish conurbations on all sides.

Nonetheless, it was in the 'basin' of Sheffield that Ethel's life and work began, and it was the 'drab affair' of northern industrial existence that gave rise to a fateful meeting at Endcliffe Vale House on 7 May 1924 where twelve prominent local citizens met to discuss forming a society to preserve local scenery, the origins of what would become the Sheffield Association for the Protection of Rural Scenery, a movement which would shapeshift and morph into something vastly influential, tenacious as its founder.

Even trying to find Ethel's birthplace is elusive: Google Maps thinks it is across the road from where it is, points to the tended detached houses behind Endcliffe Park, a pocket of woodland and water in the south-west of the city, just off trendy, ever-evolving Ecclesall Road with its student housing and microbreweries, burger restaurants and lash extension salons.

I start off in the park, the cafe with its outdoor seating and cheerful tannoy announcements. *Coffee for Mark. Food order for Dev.* It's the middle of the day, a weekday, and the paths are busy with pushchairs, spaniels with lop-sided tongues, small children learning to ride bikes and scooters, careering away from their sprinting parents. Other than Graves Park, this is one of the largest green spaces in Sheffield and it's a hotspot for joggers, duck-feeders, a solemn group practising t'ai chi, moving in slow motion watched over by the stern Queen Victoria monument. Where the path forks, there's a tree that looks like a hand waiting to cup something.

The path climbs steeply to the right through denser trees with the duck pond placid on my left. This is the bit of the park that always feels quieter, more undiscovered, home to memorials and empty benches and the makings of secret dens. There's a young beech tree on my left and I pass under the canopy of leaves. Some of them are spinning slowly to the ground, seasonal confetti. To my right, I see new builds poking above the treeline. This is a hugely desirable part of town to live in, an expensive part, close enough to the city centre but enticingly near to the route to Derbyshire. On nearby Rustlings Road, the houses cost a small fortune. For some reason, the birdsong always seems louder here than in any other place in Sheffield. It mingles with the barking of dogs. Their yapping undertone only serves to bring out the melody, a sense of lifting sweetness. There's a network of exposed tree roots on my right. Something indecorous about it, like veins too visible through skin. There are blackberry bushes clamouring for attention as I leave the park and pass through a narrow gap in the wall to join Riverdale Road, its name almost elfin, magical. It is a wrench to leave, to step back into suburbia.

Riverdale Road rises gently, detached houses with large front gardens and the new builds of the Bluebell flats, glassy and open. Soon, it meets Endcliffe Vale Road. I pause in front of the large black gates of The Lodge on my left. It looks like a fitting dwelling for Ethel, a remnant from a bygone era, auditioning to be her family home. But I know this is not my destination. I'm surrounded by University of Sheffield signs now, an insignia that denotes mass ownership, student accommodation. I leave the road and walk towards the heart of the student village where Endcliffe Vale House itself no longer stands.

There is a secrecy to the way the trees lean in here. The lawns are healthy and the grass is being mown. A blue plaque to commemorate Ethel's life stands in a corner, though I have to squint at a map to find it. The plaque unveils itself near to a rowan, flanked by a neat square hedge. It is squat under a tree that will soon be shedding conkers everywhere, showering down on her memory. The blue disc that bears the coordinates of her life is on a triangular jut of rock, facing towards the Peak District. It gestures to moorland, suggests it by its very presence here beside the student amenities. To reach the Peak from here on foot, Ethel could have taken several routes, but the one I favour would retrace my steps to the comfort of Endcliffe Park, to the ribbon of the Porter, and follow that spooling stream to Bingham Park and then into the woods as everything becomes more open towards Forge Dam, the path that climbs strenuously towards Ringinglow Road and then on to Lady Canning's Plantation and the promise of Burbage, a climbers' playground.

Endcliffe Vale is where Ethel lived and worked. If Sheffield is the crucible of England, this was the crucible of her activism. The billiard room here would become the offices of the Sheffield branch of the CPRE. It was her workplace and her family home. But now it is a tangible absence. It is overwritten each day by the footsteps of students, young hopefuls studying architecture and history, engineering and science, some of them oblivious to the very idea of the woman who dreamed and wrote here. They scurry over the blueprints, the foundations, on their way to dinner and vodka and dates, unencumbered by the past, as young people should be.

This is not where Ethel took her first breaths in 1894, but it's where she spent most of her days. She was born in Millhouses Lane, south-west Sheffield, one of five children. I am wallowing in the facts of her life again, imagining they give a fuller picture than the conkers suspended above me and the steadfast crimson of the rowan. It is a very blue kind of day,

Mr. T. W. Ward.

Ethel's mother and father: Thomas William Ward (1853–1926) and Mary Sophia Ward, née Bassett (1863–1955). © PictureSheffield.com

kite weather. Out in the Hope Valley, paragliders will be moving slowly in the air over Mam Tor, their scale reduced by distance so that you could forget for a moment that they are people, trusting and suspended. It seems like a day for seeing things from above, for perspective.

Ethel was born into wealth made from the proceeds of industry, no matter what her views on the 'drabness' of city life and its impoverishment compared to the countryside may have become. Her father was the scrap-metal-merchant-done-good Thomas W. Ward and her mother was Mary Sophia Bassett, of liquorice fame: predictably, far less is known about her maternal side, other than the connection to Trebor Bassett sweets. Thomas Ward's rise to prominence, however, is the stuff of legend, almost film-worthy. Jean Smart, secretary to the Sheffield branch of CPRE in Ethel's latter years, describes him as a 'Victorian Alan Sugar'. He was born in Sheffield in 1853 and started work at the age of fifteen as a coal merchant. With his rudimentary horse and cart, he was soon drawn into the Sheffield steel industry, catering for the huge demand for scrap metal in the 1870s. Here, he discovered an aptitude for ship breaking. Ward leased ships to the government during the Boer War. He owned breakers' yards at ports around Britain and became known for his resourceful nature, recycling almost every aspect of the warships and redundant luxury liners given over to his care, down to lamps and carpets, even timber (used for garden furniture).

There's something fascinating about Ethel's father being such a resourceful converter of goods, a nineteenth-century up-cycler, disliking waste. But Ward was also busy building his own empire: Thos. W. Ward Ltd was established in 1878 and formed into a limited company at the Albion Works in Sheffield in 1904. At the outbreak of the First World War, the company was feeding a thousand tons of scrap metal per day into Britain's steel industry, which was crucial to the nation's war effort. At the time, the horses that would usually have transported scrap metal had been requisitioned by the military to serve in Europe. It was then that Ward made the remarkable decision to lease an elephant from a menagerie at the Wicker Arches, owned by William Sedgwick. Since circus animals found themselves suddenly superfluous in wartime, it was a solution with double advantage.

An elephant, shy by the banks of the Don, patrolling through the din at Attercliffe. Known as Lizzie, Ward's requisitioned elephant is often pictured with straps across her huge back, lugging the wooden struts of a cart, surrounded by men in flat caps and jackets who seem diminished beside her proud height and bearing, trunk curled neatly underneath her, a furled banner. Lizzie was strong enough to do the work of three horses. She plodded between factories, up slopes and over cobbles, helping to stoke the city furnaces. Each night she rested in her stable at Lady's Bridge. She became a Sheffield celebrity, unlikely as summer snow, but purposeful, intent on ordinary work. She has also become the stuff of local mythology, said to have eaten a careless schoolboy's cap and pushed her trunk through kitchen windows to help herself to pies left cooling near the sill. An article reporting on the death of William Sedgwick's son Richard, in 1931, mentions that while Lizzie was working in South Yorkshire, an engine got stuck in the snow and Lizzie was called to the rescue, successfully pulling it out. She appears in anecdotes and articles as a kind of lumbering South Yorkshire Lassie, there to help the residents of Sheffield in times of need, until her retirement, possibly induced by the effects of the hard, uneven Sheffield streets on her feet.

It's difficult to square the image of a pie-thieving elephant with the industrious, somewhat pious character of Thomas Ward. A stern Methodist, Ward surrounded himself with like-minded people who were well off but interested in projects he considered 'worthy', such as building chapels. He was close friends with Alderman J.G. Graves, an apprentice watchmaker who became one of Sheffield's most significant benefactors and would be vital to Ethel's later preservation efforts. Ethel may have learned something of the importance of networking from her parents, but it was underlined by her education. She and her younger sister Gertie (nicknamed 'Gag' by the rest of the family) were sent to boarding school just outside London at West Heath, Kent, later attended by Diana Spencer.

Lizzie Ward (elephant), working for Thomas W. Ward, Albion Works. © PictureSheffield.com

Picture an eighteenth-century building with cloisters and pillars at the entrance, built in cheerful beige stone. Here, they mixed with young women from wealthy and aristocratic backgrounds. Ethel said of their experience at the school, 'all we had was money'. The absent (but implied) word here is 'new'. Ethel and Gertie were without the extensive connections and sense of entitlement that perhaps accompanies decades or even centuries of inherited wealth, the significance of a known name, an intricate system of friendships and connections. 'All' they had was money. But 'all' is something. Ethel went on to read English at university in London. By the time she returned to Sheffield in 1913, her father had been appointed the Master Cutler of Sheffield, head of the Hallamshire Company of Cutlers and an ambassador for industry in the city, a prestigious historic role created in 1624, a reflection of his standing and significance. Endcliffe Vale House was commissioned and built as a symbol of Ward's largesse: a grand mansion by the park, solid as his legacy.

With one eye always fixed on the future, Thomas Ward set up a trust fund for his daughters. Income from this would ensure a comfortable life for them, but the capital from it could not be spent. It was a security net from which all kinds of later radicalism and philanthropy could proceed. The preservation of the Peak District was enabled by fortunes built on sugar and scrap.

Perhaps we prefer narratives of working-class trailblazing: the ramblers anticipated and commemorated in Ewan MacColl's song 'The Manchester Rambler', the Young Communist League snaking their way from Hayfield to the top of Kinder Scout in 1932, the embodiment of the struggle for the right to roam against the rights of the wealthy to have exclusive access to the moors for grouse shooting. Perhaps this is why Ethel's work – so much more genteel, so much more bureaucratic, proceeding in offices and through letters and persuasive conversations – is not the stuff of ballads and poetry; why her life has been the subject of scant discussion, even in the city that owes so much to her. It is so much less filmic. It comes with chauffeurs and housekeepers, the rituals of afternoon tea and dressing for dinner. It is contradictory. But Ward's foresight and his entrepreneurial spirit endowed Ethel with the means to pursue her passions, to go to university and read the work of the Romantic poets, to begin to align her memory of the countryside which surrounded her suburban childhood home with the demands being made by Wordsworth and Coleridge for a poetry, a way of living, which would recognise the interdependence of human beings and nature. As a student, Ethel would certainly have read the preface to the *Lyrical Ballads*, with its strident defence of the importance of creative expression and its focus on the reciprocal relationship between man and nature. According to the preface, a poet:

> considers man and nature as essentially adapted to each other, and the mind of man as naturally the mirror of the fairest and most interesting properties of nature … The knowledge both of the Poet and the Man of Science is pleasure; but the knowledge of the one cleaves to us as a necessary part of our existence, our natural and unalienable inheritance; the other is a personal and individual acquisition, slow to come to us, and by no habitual and direct sympathy connecting us with our fellow-beings. The Man of Science seeks truth as a remote and unknown benefactor; he cherishes and loves it in his solitude: the Poet, singing a song in which all human beings join with him, rejoices in the presence of truth as our visible friend and hourly companion. Poetry is the breath and finer spirit of all knowledge …

I almost hear an echo of that sentiment in Ethel's 1962 article on 'Living in Sheffield':

> The saving of the countryside itself is the most vital thing for the souls and bodies of its inhabitants.

I imagine Ethel reading Romantic poetry in her early days in the London of 1910, a woman free in the city, contemplating Wordsworth's description of stealing a boat in *The Prelude*, overlooked by 'a huge peak, black and huge' and thinking of the life ahead of her with a similar feeling of vertigo and thrill. To celebrate her return from university, her mother decided to take her on a three-month visit to Paris. That trip would irrevocably alter the course of her life.

Ethel at home.

Sheffield, summer 2023

Dear Ethel (I know, I know, I have dispensed with formalities),

I am looking for you in old film reels. Most of them are so brief, if I look away for a second I've missed them. This one has a jolly title: *The Freedom of the Hills: Thousands of ramblers gather at Winnats Pass*. Here are grayscale hills. Black, white and grey bodies. Men scrambling uphill over tufts of grass, using their hands. At times, it's as if they're clambering over each other.

    Now there are bodies vaulting a drystone wall. A woman in a jacket and skirt hesitates, waiting until last. She has dark hair, cropped close in a bob, just like you. Eventually, a man with an open shirt and a cigarette in his mouth offers her a hand and she's over, disappearing from the frame. Then, swarms of people. Seen from above they seem to be growing from the sides of Winnats Pass, emerging from the earth, where they've been buried along with the ghost stories, the couple who ran away and met their death here on the slopes at the hands of greedy miners, the first journeys through this winding landscape when the hills beyond Castleton must have seemed impenetrable. Applause. Fade out.

    I know it wasn't you I glimpsed there. But I think you'd enjoy the way I'm looking for you, raking through footage and photographs, finding scant evidence of your face. You'd approve, I think, because it means I'm studying the face of the Peak District properly, altering the sketches in my mind, making them more complicated.

    BBC footage of Peak District ramblers. Women walking in tweeds. Men with hands in their pockets. A jaunty and excitable spaniel. Everyone is sticking to the path (I don't know where the path is), but a child strikes off alone and hares up a bank. Two women sitting, the wind running invisible hands through their hair. A view towards an outcrop, bordered by shadowy trees. I love the grainy aspect. It makes me think of my granddad in Oldham, alone in front of his small black and white TV set, patient, staring at it until he seemed to become monochrome himself. He never replaced it with a colour TV. Perhaps he liked the way it lent each landscape an intensity of depth and texture, the distraction of brightness removed. There is the Peak District in bloom and then there is this preserved version, all etched with light and dark, a moving linocut.

    Why do we need a human face for everything? Why do I need to see you to make sense of everything you did? When we write, we can speak to people without them having to see us. Am I offending your anonymity? Would you like me to step away from the desk and listen to the rain tap-dancing on the roof of the shed instead? Don't answer that. I already know what you'd say. And you're right. Ethel, you're always right.

    Yours,
    Helen

'To be married tomorrow,' Miss E.M.B. Ward, daughter of Mr and Mrs T.W. Ward, of Endcliffe Vale House, Sheffield, and Lieutenant W.B. Gallimore, West Riding Royal Field Artillery. From the *Sheffield Daily Telegraph*, 25 February 1916. © PictureSheffield.com

Aching Delight

Terrible is our love and sad,
Passionate and boundless glad,
Like Bowfell's fierce flowing fountains
Eternal and youth renewing
Like the great eagles wooing
On the heights, on the Cumbrian mountains.
(from 'An Offering' by Henry Burrows Gallimore)

After Ethel emerged from university and her immersion in the literary classics, Paris must have seemed dangerous, exciting. In the Louvre and in the heady atmosphere of the Left Bank, Ethel fell more deeply in love with art and literature. Having let poetry into her heart, its incantations, she was soon to fall wildly, dangerously in love with a poet.

Henry Burrows Gallimore was from Sheffield steel stock too. Nearly ten years older than Ethel, he worked for his father's cutlery company, Gallimore and Sons, and had read languages at Cambridge University, lodging by the imposing crenellated spires of King's College in the stately heart of the city. In the few existing pictures of him, he's slim and upright with a long face, strong chin, a large but trimmed moustache. He and Ethel were married in 1916. It was to prove tragically brief.

Henry and Ethel's passionate romance seems fixed, preserved in the valleys of the Lake District, flush with rain, the mountains where they honeymooned. And their love is held in the pages of 'An Offering', a long, meandering, breathless poem written by Henry and finished and printed later by Ethel. How much she added to the original is unknown; the early passages are marked with a single asterisk and the back of the book bears a neat note: 'I found these verses by my husband left incomplete. I have tried to complete them.' The poem is a kind of restless, shape-shifting love story, moving between the moors of the Peak District and the imposing fells of Cumbria. It reads as a call-and-response between two lovers, both fearful and ecstatic, but also between those human voices of the northern English landscape. The American-Irish poet Michael Donaghy once described a poem as 'a diagram of consciousness'. Since we know relatively little of Henry Gallimore's character, 'An Offering' is his embodiment. If it is a 'diagram' of his consciousness, it is a complex, overwritten one, sketched in a state of heightened emotion. It is less Wordsworth's 'emotion recollected in tranquility' and more 'emotion crashing through tranquility'. It is turbulent and celebratory. It burns fiercely, is deeply felt.

From its first pages, 'An Offering' paints a sensuous and dramatic portrait of a Lake District suffused with the brooding passions of the two young lovers. A lake is not placid but 'scented, calm, voluptuous'. Birds sing 'all drunken'. The Langdale Pikes are compared to a bride and bridegroom, standing proud together. Cumbria seems teeming with life, and no detail goes unnoticed: the intricacies of paths leading towards Grasmere, the 'quiet islands' of Rydal, full of shining stones 'with holes the waters had born'. The world brims with 'aching delight' and 'wild, sweet pain'. Everything is tinged with the sensibility of new romance:

And in the sun, like immortality
Fold upon fold, pikes and dim crags and screes,
Mounts of tumultuous love and poetry

Landscape in the poetry and poetry in the landscape: the tangible, brooding presence of words and verses, the shadow cast by language and the savage grandeur of its music. Often expressions of love for the land ('my beautiful dark land', 'my passionate bare land') mingle with the intimacy between the two characters. There's an almost physical sense of need in the pages, a bristling desire. Wanting distorts all sense of time, and the poem has a feel of existing outside of time, suspended. When the lovers finally touch one another, the electricity is palpable:

Love's waiting hours are months and years of pain
And when he came speechless we stood with bliss
Then clasped as we might ne'er clasp again
And kissed as though life hung upon a kiss.

Ethel and Henry kissing on the summit of Loughrigg, all of Grasmere Vale steeped in watercolour, fluid orange light below them. Ethel and Henry pressing their faces together as if each could absorb the imprint of the other. Dancing slowly, pointlessly, beside Easedale Tarn for no audience. Finding the hidden places, the spots less obvious than caves and waterfalls, and cleaving to each other, memorising each other, the scent of bracken and sweat, the sweetness of each other. Ethel and Henry squeezing hands by the prehistoric stones in Langdale, the imprints in the rock. Imagining they could imprint themselves with such giddying permanence, become part of the scenery.

The poem is divided into sections and that only heightens the sense of drama, of 'scenes' being played out. It builds towards a crescendo. A sense of encroaching threat develops; the lovers' wonder at the world they are exploring is tinged with premonition:

It was that silent, ominous, scented calm
That hangs over the hushed garden ere the thunder

Soon after, there's a first mention of war, of the skies' 'hurtling battles' and of nations massing, gathering. There's a faint hope that love will triumph, that 'love's rage is wilder than the rage of war'. But there is a pained separation to confront, the young man called up to fight. Having merged, the two are dragged apart with sudden force.

In an awful moment of prophecy, the lonely young woman who has been left to roam the moors without her lover is out walking one day when she's summoned home. Her first thought is that it must be her returning man. Instead, she comes face to face with his friend who tells her, 'you must be brave', and then reveals, 'your lover was killed yesterday at noon'. She refuses to believe the news. It must be a mistake. She denies and denies, while the soldier remains steadfast. 'And then,' she says, 'the storm broke over me.'

Captain Henry Gallimore was part of the 312th Brigade, Royal Field Artillery. He was killed in France in 1917, aged thirty-one. He and Ethel had been married for just fifteen months. His grave is near Arras.

The storm was not breaking over Ethel, it was inside her. It raged the way a fever does. She was just twenty-two and already a widow. She'd forged a new world of experience with Henry, run wild with him over the Lakeland fells, cold water on her skin, rain in her hair, then that world, that life was brutally extinguished. She was alone in Sheffield, surrounded by her family but utterly isolated. She lost weight and her nerves were frayed. She sought solace in the war poetry of Wilfred Owen, but his ability to expose the futility of battle must have been scant comfort, his disavowal of the 'old lie', '*Dulce et decorum est / Pro patria mori*', the dictum that it is sweet and fitting to die for one's country.

His poem 'Futility', perhaps his most devastating, opens with the narrator urging that a dead soldier be dragged into the warmth of the sun, a last hopeful act ('If anything might rouse him now / The kind old sun will know.'), but it ends in bitter desperation: if we are in the business of killing and maiming each other, 'what made fatuous sunbeams toil to break earth's sleep at all?' There is a sense in Owen's work of the earth itself revolting at the barbarities of war. Ethel turned to William Blake too, to his scepticism of organised religion, his profound joys and deeper griefs, the way he noticed 'marks of wisdom, marks of woe' in the faces of strangers by the banks of the Thames. Poetry was an amplification of her feelings, a place where she could recognise her despair, incomprehension and anger. But it was not exactly a distraction from mourning. Ethel sleepwalked through her days in Sheffield, profoundly marked by what had been stolen from her so suddenly.

In that raw aftermath, Ethel also turned to seances, hoping she could speak with her lost love. Spiritualism was in vogue by the end of the war, prompted by the mass-scale losses. We are more likely to believe in ghosts after such wholesale slaughter. Celebrity and literary figures like Arthur Conan Doyle had done much to popularise it too. Conan Doyle was a physician, but towards the end of his life he was a fervent believer in the paranormal, perhaps triggered by his son Kingsley and younger brother Innes both surviving the First World War, only to die of influenza. Conan Doyle was a great friend of the escape artist Harry Houdini and regularly attended seances (which, ironically, ended the friendship: Conan Doyle's second wife, Jean Leckie, offended Houdini at one such gathering by claiming she could channel the spirit of Houdini's dead mother, producing reams of automatic writing which he considered bogus). As a renowned writer, Ethel would no doubt have held Conan Doyle in high regard.

But more significantly, it's likely that Henry Gallimore himself was interested in the supernatural and the idea of communicating with the dead, seeing it as aligned with his poetry: there is an account of a seance contained in 'An Offering', a glass which moves, a name spelled out. Though a Methodist by upbringing, grief had flung the doors of perception wide for Ethel.

She was greatly affected by the seances she attended and once believed that Henry (or Harry as she called him) was speaking to her from the afterlife. This was a small and temporary comfort. The silence that followed must have been deafening.

For all its anguish, there is hope in the final pages of 'An Offering'. Though separated in life, the young lovers are to be reunited in heaven ('the culmination of all life'). The last words of the poem are fiercely sexual, sex and death merging together: 'to-night he leads me to the marriage bed'. There is a sense of redemption and possibility and, unsurprisingly, this finds its expression through the landscape. In this case, not the Lake District but the peaks of Derbyshire:

If there is any healing, here I come,
Warm fragrant moors and the steep freshening streams
Where wild bees through the purple heather hum
As beauteous through the soul immortal dreams.
The old blown agin gives his rough heart's ease,
Great curlews all night cry where I do rest.
Take me, O Mother Cap, to thy rugged knees,
O lone and star crowned Mam Tor to thy breast

It is unclear whether it is the dead soldier here speaking from his grave, or whether it is the lover left behind who hopes for healing. Either way, it's clear that redemption is to be found in wildness, in the harsh, unforgiving elements (elements that might yet forgive) and the jagged points that interrupt the Derbyshire moors. Ethel's sister Gertie felt the wisdom of this idea acutely. As Ethel mourned, Gertie began to plan outings for them. She would get their chauffeur to take the whole family out to places like Hathersage and Bamford, the picturesque villages of the Hope Valley, sitting just beneath the shelter of the gritstone edges. Sometimes they'd go to the Longshaw Estate or to Dovedale, further south. Sometimes it was just Gertie and Ethel, the sisters facing adventure together, as they had done at boarding school, two of them against the world.

Perhaps Gertie knew that her sister would be distracted not just by the sheer abundance of the 'beautiful frame' but by evidence of human encroachment on it. This was a time of change and development. Petrol stations had sprung up along roadsides, and along with them came advertisement hoardings, litter and the groundwork for ribbon developments of new homes. Ethel began to feel irritated by the intrusion of what she called 'cuckoo's egg' houses – 'ugly' one-off new builds in elegant villages like Hathersage, designs that stood out a mile. This was the era before the 1947 Town and Country Planning Act, when people who owned land could build whatever they wished on it. She was angry, indignant. The countryside she was just getting to know was being spoiled. She had got some of her passion back. A resolve was forming and Gertie could sense it.

Ethel would later describe the redemptive power of this difficult period of life in her poem *The Pride of the Peak*:

My years arose a black and starless wall,
And begged to cease before each loathed morrow
Upon their hungriness should fall.
And after this Thou struckst my body low
With hideous jangled nerves and ceaseless pain
From nature all unfilled and grieving slow,
That only earth's high beauties held me sane.

This is a remarkable passage for a modern audience to read. The 'black and starless wall' is a stark embodiment of depression. Not only is the narrator here openly acknowledging suicidal thoughts ('begged to cease before each loathed morrow'), but the whole tenor of the stanza is not dissimilar to the kind of sentiments we might see on social media today, in Instagram posts that celebrate the importance of the outdoors to mental health. The suffering evoked here is physical; it's in the body as well as the 'jangled nerves'. Slow grief is only relieved by hills and mountains, by the 'high beauties' found in nature. Ethel's writing seems candidly ahead of its time. Or perhaps, like the passionate and anguished lines of 'An Offering', her words exist out of time.

A belief was forming in Ethel, one in sympathy with the spirit of 'An Offering' and its hope for healing. The English countryside could have a redemptive power. The world was in turmoil, but landscape was a constant friend, a witness and confidante. It could be the 'new Jerusalem' that William Blake had written of, a place of solace and inspiration for war heroes to return to. But it required guardians, champions who would fight for it.

By early 1924, Ethel, now thirty, was writing letters to the 'great and good' of Sheffield – she knew many of them personally – urging them to form a committee with her to safeguard the Peak District. She wanted to gauge interest, gather like-minded philanthropists around her as her father had done before her. Her first action was small but significant. Walking by the Fox House pub, she had noticed many people getting off buses at the stop there and immediately shedding ticket stubs. She wrote a letter to the Sheffield bus company persuading them to fit buses with a ticket receptacle to prevent bus tickets being littered across the Peak. They agreed. She was getting things done.

In the seven years since Henry's death, she had undergone slow change. It was imperceptible at first, gradual as the grasses growing taller by the bank at Padley Gorge, the bracken's blanket thinning in winter. Now, she had a private purpose which she could express through public endeavour. She must protect all that she could. She must build the idyll those early walks in the Lake District had shown to her. As if Henry might still return and wait for her at Robin Hood's cave, his shape silhouetted, barely distinguishable from the outlines of the rocks.

In the middle of 'An Offering', there's a poem which stands alone, a love poem addressed to a woman 'sweeter than all sweet dames of history'. Looking down the side of the page, it reveals itself to be an acrostic. The letters spell EMBGALLIMORE.

Whenever, Wherever

Dear Ethel,

8 a.m.

Did you have nicknames we don't know about? Did you dream in the language of gritstone? Did you keep your walking boots clean at all times, or did you let them cake with mud? How many cups of tea did you drink each morning? What was the first thing you said when you woke up? If pushed, which had your heart, the White Peak or the Dark? Did the war leave its tidemark on you? What did you push to the back of the house's highest shelf? What would you say if you were writing this book yourself?

11 a.m.

I'm sorry for my earlier impertinence. There are peonies and dog roses in the garden at the moment, both shades of pink, and I've picked a peony for you, all frothy petals and clean soap scent. Then I put gloves on and grappled with some thistles and I stuffed them in a vase beside it. They look terrible together, but I like what they symbolise. The morning's already unravelling. It's going to be a hot day, a drying day, and I'm thinking of all the walkers across Derbyshire topping up their water bottles and setting out, not knowing when they'll next find shade. I hope you'll forgive my questions. I hope you'll forgive this clumsy flower, how I've angled it towards the window, south-west facing, so it can dream of edges.

12 p.m.

On the screen, a steam train is bisecting an industrial town. The steam billows, its movement almost liquid. Like tracks in cream when it's being whipped. It is beautiful and terrifying, how the train changes the sky. The backs of terraces. Football. Life, its gentle oblivion. That sense of gathering change, gathering pace.

1 p.m.

I do wonder though: what kind of pen did you write with?

Yours hopelessly,
Helen

Longshaw
Sheep-dog
trials.

Glad is the old rock, Mother Cap,
On a morning of the year,
When blossoms gay her feet o'erwrap,
And dogs and shepherds near;
In bright September weather,
When folk come all together
Under the brilliant heather
Beside the Longshaw meer.

A stanza from Ethel's handwritten manuscript of *The Pride of the Peak* (see page 148).

Longshaw and Blacka Moor

In bright September weather,
When folk come all together
Under the brilliant heather
Beside the Longshaw meer.
(The Pride of the Peak)

7 May 1924. Early summer, the days not yet stupefied by heat. An energetic time of year, barely removed from the fizz and promise of spring. Ethel's family home at Endcliffe Vale House in the quiet, south-western suburbs of Sheffield was playing host to a momentous gathering of twelve. Gathered around her, a cross-section of those considered to be Sheffield's leading citizens: academics, representatives of industry, physicians. There were architects and historians, antiquaries and archivists. Gertie, Ethel's sister, was present and so was her brother, Alan Ward. And somewhere in the room, in a shadow-stippled corner, the spirit of Henry Gallimore, quietly observing, noticed only by Ethel.

The aims of the people assembled were simple and vast: they were combining their powers to preserve 'local scenery' and protect the land around the city of Sheffield. But first, there were administrative matters to settle. Most pressingly, they needed to identify specific goals and to decide what to call themselves. The latter of these aims would prove no mean feat. Sir Henry Hadow, vice-chancellor of the University of Sheffield, was proposed and seconded as president of the fledgling society, and Ethel, instigator of the meeting, was elected honorary secretary. Their aim of finding an apt name would not be resolved until several meetings later: first they were to be a society, then a 'committee'. Names: so natural once established, so difficult to choose. They toyed with the idea of being the 'Sheffield & District Vigilance Committee of the National Trust'; the word 'vigilance' seems apt, in line with Ethel's watchfulness, her commitment to noticing. In 1925, they settled on the 'Sheffield Association for the Protection of Local Scenery'.

Simultaneously, the Council for the Preservation of Rural England was being formed in London. They invited the group to affiliate with them, and this invitation was accepted in 1927, unanimously approved.

The mood was no doubt buoyant but cautious. In those formative meetings, representatives of the new Sheffield wing of CPRE rallied against the perceived threats posed by development, focusing on environmental change instigated by social changes. The modernisation of the 1920s saw increased car ownership and the rise of the 'day trip', touring the countryside in vehicles. To cope with demand, there were proposals for road widening, bridge replacements, electricity pylons – the landscape of my youth in North East Derbyshire, chains and chains of them, like huge metal scarecrows – quarries and factories, bold roadside advertisements. At that very first gathering at Endcliffe Vale, members were indignant about the proposed construction of a road through Winnats Pass, the forbidding, imposing, craggy limestone gorge west of Castleton, overlooked by Mam Tor.

It is worth taking a moment to imagine Ethel's unusual position as a woman in this new committee structure. As Matthew Kelly puts it in his depiction of pioneering female environmental activists:

> In the nineteenth and twentieth centuries, activist women were often caricatured as eccentric, unflatteringly referred to as blue stockings or dismissed as upper-class busybodies, theatrical figures who were a bit posh, a bit barmy, with nothing better to do than bother the authorities with shrill claims that failed to grasp realities. When a man says 'that bloody woman', to use a mild form of the demotic, he almost always means a woman who has trespassed on what he takes to be his domain or who has challenged masculine authority.

Furthermore, there may have been differences in approach between male and female committee members:

> Their work was not understood to be 'women's work' – plenty of men did committee work in this period – but their status as women was central to their experiences and, in some cases, how they conceived of their work. Advantages and disadvantages were conferred by being, so to speak, the only woman in the room.

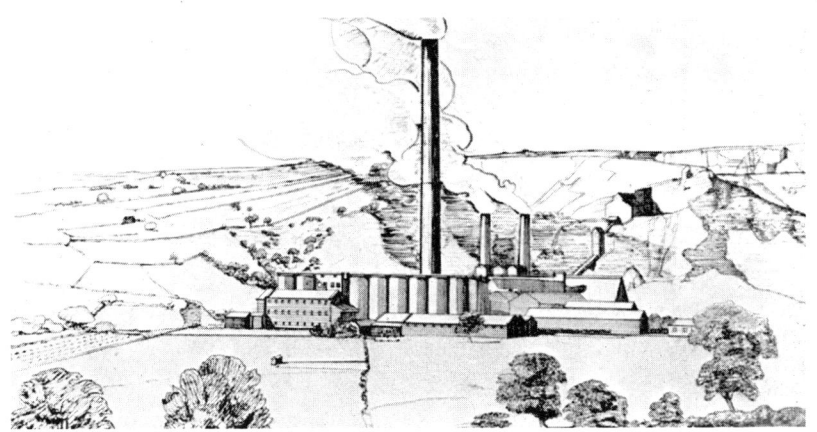

A visualisation of the impact of G&T Earle's cement works at Hope – an early target of CPRE's campaigning.

He argues it gave them licence to challenge existing mores and assumptions, even though it could be very isolating.

Ethel understood the power of metaphor. The early passions of Sheffield's rural defenders, and Ethel in particular, might best be symbolised by a clutch of litter displayed at Cutlers' Hall in Sheffield city centre in September 1929. A glass case, brimming with empty fruit tins, cigarette ends and matchboxes, chocolate wrappers, broken bottles and what the *Sheffield Daily Telegraph* described as 'an indescribable heap of filthy paper'. The name of this startling exhibit was 'What Sheffield Left at Stanage Last Bank Holiday'. Ethel was preoccupied with the intrusion of the city into the countryside, and littering vividly symbolised this. The cabinet was part of an exhibition called 'Save the Countryside', originally displayed in Leicester at a preservation of the countryside exhibition in 1928. But Ethel knew that to make people care, there would need to be a local component, a series of photographs and items that would bring home to Sheffielders the threat to their Peak District 'in some striking pictorial form'. This might be seen as the beginning of the group's persuasive use of visual imagery and the involvement of talented local amateur photographer Phil Barnes, a rambler with an intimate knowledge of Derbyshire and a keen eye for a tableau. In his image of Win Hill from Kinder Scout, shadow is as important as light. The hill seems lapped by it. We sense something encroaching, overlapping. A visual metaphor for the connection between city and open land. The *Sheffield Daily Telegraph* concluded that the exhibition, attended by some 4,000 people, was powerful, effective in showing 'not only how things were being done wrong, but how they could be done right'.

Phil Barnes had joined CPRE in 1928, but in 1929 became assistant secretary (a salaried position). His photographic work is compelling: in 1934 he published a book called *Trespassers Will Be Prosecuted*, which illustrated the problem of lack of access to some areas of the Peak District through striking visual imagery. His meticulous photographs, combined with his intimate knowledge of Derbyshire, were an asset to the group.

Some of the feared developments which troubled Ethel in those early years could not reasonably be stopped. Anyone who has ever climbed at Stanage Edge will have noticed the incongruity of the Hope cement works, pale against the skyline. I once sheltered under a lip of rock with a man who was out there casually soloing in his jeans, shimmying up tough overhangs with fluency, and we paused there, letting the showers pass, watched a bird of prey hover directly above the factory chimney, wobbling elegantly on a current of breeze. It was a strange and powerful juxtaposition. The cement works almost seem a timeless feature of that view from Stanage now, strangely fitting, despite the stark contrast with the rolling hills. I cannot imagine the Hope Valley without it. In a 1927 meeting of CPRE, it was noted that, 'opposition to the erection of the works would be useless but ... certain concessions to scenery might be demanded'. This seems to have taken the form of seeded banks and tree planting. The cement works themselves have become a fixture.

In those early days, Ethel's role was intense and often rather solitary: she had to use her foresight and funds to buy up Peak properties herself; Upper Booth in Edale was perhaps the most timely example of this. But her crowning achievement concerned a huge swathe of land known as Longshaw.

There's something infinitely friendly about the Longshaw Estate these days. As you approach from the car park, the bridge seems to extend a welcome. I set off towards Padley Gorge on well-maintained paths. There are cheerful National Trust signposts everywhere. I run along the first wide track, koala coloured. There are walks signed everywhere, orange and red arrows. As soon as I'm through the first gate, there's a huge millstone dedicated to the estate. It says thank you to all who have dedicated their time since 1927, and there are carvings of hands everywhere. This part of the path feels enchanted, and I often come here with my son to hide and seek among the trees. There are rhododendrons everywhere and their branches braid around each other,

SAVED FOR THE NATION

THE LONGSHAW ESTATE
765 acres purchased for the National Trust by public subscription, 1927—1931
By courtesy of "The Times"

An illustration of an early campaign success – saving Longshaw – from the pamphlet 'A Joint Appeal to Save the Beauty of Derbyshire and the Peak' (c.1935).

twisting and turning. It creates the feeling of a magical wood, otherworldly. Even on a rainy day with hardly anyone about, there are small birds darting. A magpie takes off, startled by my intrusion. There are signs explaining how to properly close the gates. Open land. A body of water, calm, to my right. It always feels cultivated here, protected, well-managed, even down to the large logs that have been draped across the little stream running on my left, the flagstones. There are bubbles in the puddles from the force of rain, a little blackbird almost skipping on the path in front of me.

I skirt around the water, head towards Yarncliffe. There are huge, felled trees, something beached-whale about them. So many routes and all of them inviting. Ducks skim down and land on the water as one, and others plop down from the bank and join them. They're those beautiful, multicoloured showy ducks with bands of russet, teal and ochre on them. Even the ducks are decorous. Decadent. And now there are crows. When do they become a murder? Is three only a manslaughter of crows? They detonate from the trees and go upwards into mist. On the ground everywhere there are husks. Signs, keeping me vigilant. *Lift latch and open gate. Dogs on leads, please.* A squirrel shimmies dextrously down from higher branches and finds a different tree to shin up, making movement look easy. I imagine other kinds of creatures, unknown to me, unnamed to me, darting into the undergrowth.

Early hand-drawn posters by P.B. Fischer for a campaigning lantern talk in Hathersage (left: Surprise View; right: Stanage Edge, looking south).

Whenever I come to Longshaw, it feels too fleeting. I want to come back at night, climb like a squirrel, and hide here with the knuckled branches. *Protect the invisible. Keep your dog on a lead. Protect nesting chicks. This is particularly important between March and July. Cows with calves graze in this area. Cattle can feel threatened by dogs, especially when they are with their calves. If you feel you may be chased, let go of the lead.* There are places here where the hillside has eroded, bowls scooped out, guarded by trees. The branches reach down and brush the floor as if they're tidying it, the way everything seems tidy at Longshaw. I have a memory of this path from when I was young, from what seemed to be interminable walks in the Peak District with my dad. I always had the tantalising sense of almost knowing where I was, but not quite. And now that I know, now that I could pinpoint a location on a map, I want to go back to that state of not knowing. Such is being human. There are hillocks, tufty bits of grass. Here is a crossroads; Longshaw is full of them. It feels like a gateway to the Peak.

The name Longshaw is said to derive from the long wood in Padley Gorge, above Grindleford. Today, it is arguably one of the most popular places in the national park. But it could so easily have become private land without public access, had Ethel and CPRE not intervened. The Longshaw Estate was owned by the Duke of Rutland; it comprised the duke's shooting lodge and 747 acres of woodlands, garden, farms and park, combined with an even vaster surrounding area of high moorland, including areas like Burbage Edge, the rocky outcrop between Stanage and the approach downhill to Sheffield. It had been acquired in 1855. In 1927, the duke put the land up for sale in order to pay death duties, with no selling restrictions imposed. This meant that, theoretically, any kind of building work could take place on it, and initial proposed ideas included detached houses, a hotel and a golf course. Representatives of CPRE were horrified by such suggestions. The local authorities of Chesterfield and Sheffield soon resolved to acquire some of the high moorlands for water catchment. Ethel and her associates' role was to help purchase the rest. It was bought for £27,000 thanks to a £13,000 bank loan, public donations and the assistance of the Corporation of Sheffield (the city council). Other members of the public subsequently donated to help the organisation pay off the loan. Ethel understood the importance of acting quickly and taking a risk. The successful purchase was also testament to the power of awareness-raising, as in the Cutlers' Hall exhibition, campaigning and relentless letter writing. The property at Longshaw was conveyed to the National Trust in 1931.

This is why I can run through a rain-slicked January on these paths. What is it about setting out in foul weather that – once you get used to it – is exhilarating? I am excited by it. As if you're seeing the things that nobody else can be bothered to notice in this hue, in this slant of light, lifted and gathered and flattened by this wind, pelted, sometimes brightened by these rains. Bad weather gives emphasis. The cold in your fingertips and the colour in your cheeks. That feeling you get in your legs as they tingle, fight to keep you warm and keep you going. This is true British winter. Not still, calm, glacial cold, but mercurial, changing elements, tardy skies, treacherous ground, tricksy forecasts. The British winter always saying, *well, what are you going to do about me then? You don't want to be out in this, do you?* But with every step, I say I do.

After my run, I drive back towards south Sheffield, but something makes me pull over and enter the empty car park at Blacka Moor. It's coming down even harder now and to go back into it seems like delightful madness. I hitch my charcoal-coloured hood over my head, heavy with water, and leave the comfort of my tin box. The sign at the entrance to the wooded area says,

Be nice, say hi. There is nobody to say hi to, so I tip my imaginary hat to imaginary Ethel, who, in my mind, has her back to the drystone wall, finding the most sheltered place, coolly observing me.

The trees don't know what to do with so much rain. They're witchy and wise, reaching skinny fingers. The visitor information board describes this place as being on the doorstep of Sheffield, made up of 180 hectares of wildlife-rich landscape. A mosaic. Hairstreak butterflies. Stone chats. Thanks in large part to Ethel's influence, J.G. Graves gave Blacka Moor to the people of Sheffield in the 1930s. None of the creatures listed on the sign are in evidence today, they're all lying low. The puddles are forming a river as I run and the road to Hathersage is loud beside me.

As I start to enter the nature reserve, there are tree roots waiting to trick me, a fast-flowing stream, spooling into the woodland, inviting me to follow. The trees lean over the path, trying to reach their opposite neighbours. My feet squelch on the path. Everything is a sort of livid green: mossy tree trunks, grass illuminated by the contrast with grey sky. Everywhere there are places to turn off, but I stick to the main path. Latticework of tree roots, progress unsteady. The inevitability of rain on the surface of the stored water. There's a bench where someone could sit a while and contemplate Blacka Moor, this patchwork. I crave more distance from the road, want to turn off. People describe paths ribboning, but this is more like a piece of brown string, the kind of thread my grandma would have used to remove a loose tooth: tie to the door and slam it. I follow the sign for a bridleway and leave the traffic behind. I can't believe that in all the years I've lived in and around Sheffield, I've never thought to stop my car here and get out before. I imagine on a clear day, from this vantage point, I could see the city. But today everything is obscured by mizzle, indistinct. Layers of trees on trees, waves of trees, crashing back towards the city. Suddenly everything opens and I can feel the presence of moor: jogging over gritstone instead of roots, everything wilder. This is the coldest, most unforgiving part of the year. You need Ethel's spirit and tenacity to still feel lifted by the more forbidding beauty instead of skittering for shelter. The ground is boggy, sucking at my shoes, which let the water in. Blacka Moor. When I repeat the name, it makes me think of ravens. Edgar Allan Poe and nevermore.

I have to cross a stream, a torrent from higher up in the Peak. The sound of it is a slow collapse. I need to jump over. That relief upon landing. Trying to gain higher ground. We always talk about mud as if it's something undifferentiated, but today I'm noticing the different qualities of it: brindled in places, some sandy and some a richer, mahogany loam, some almost rusty. Everywhere there are places where I could go crashing off through dead orange bracken if I wanted to. The moor is daring me to turn back and I'm being defiant. As I think that, my feet nearly go from under me. Gritstone rocks, like a baby's new teeth, pushing up through the damp ground. The whole moor is teething and angry.

The wind is a provocation. It tries to lift me up and send me back to Sheffield. But really, I know the wind doesn't care about me. It's busy shifting and lifting the mulch leaves, stirring the branches of the ageless trees. There's a solitary glove, foamy scum on the surface of the water. The path is a river now and I'm having to wade through it to get back to where I started. There are other paths, desire paths where people have tried to avoid the mud. How do you put a price on this boggy torpor? This vantage point? This small, cold haven of Eastern Grit?

Since 1929, Norton Rural District Council had owned the moor and resisted any planning developments. But in the early 1930s, it was coming under increased pressure: the corporation was in no financial position to pay the compensation that would have been due if permission to develop the area were repeatedly refused. Ethel decided to approach Alderman Graves, a friend of her father's. One Mr F.W. Scorah made the initial contact and then Ethel, as she put it, 'supplemented the attack'. She later recalled Graves' initial indifference to the idea of buying the land, having no apparent connection with this overlooked area of the Peak District, passed by en route to more exciting locations. Ethel knew that the lived experience of being at Blacka Moor was wholly different from the idea of the place. As she put it:

> I begged him to just go through the wood which hides the view from the main road.

There's something very plaintive and hopeful about her entreaty that I only understood after running at Blacka Moor myself. What a difference a few hundred metres of land can make, a few steps from the known into the mysterious. Graves did as Ethel had suggested:

> We learned afterwards that, on doing so, he cast his eyes over the sweep of the Black hills and said within himself 'It's mine' … A few days later I received a momentous telephone call. It was Mr Scorah who said in a quiet voice 'Graves thinks he will'. And, as you know, Graves did.

In a 1974 talk at Sheffield City Hall, Ethel would pay tribute to Alderman Graves and his remarkable foresight:

> Here was a man, self-made, without the cultural advantages no doubt, of other wealthy citizens, who yet saw what was the most priceless gift he could leave us – the saving of the countryside at our doors.

In 1933, at a public ceremony, the area of Blacka Moor was officially handed over to the city of Sheffield by Graves. He's pictured, snowy-haired and besuited, the roll of the hills tidal behind him. After the festivities, he stood with Ethel, looking out at the land.

> Now, after we've done all this for you [by 'we' he meant the Graves Trust] will you promise never to trouble us again?

I imagine Ethel's look of bemusement, half steely, half playful.

> I took a deep breath, thought I'd better be truthful and said, 'Whenever the countryside around Sheffield is in danger, I shall appeal to you.' He looked at me, severely but not unkindly. 'Well,' he said, 'now we know.'

For Ethel, the need to cause trouble had barely begun.

Alderman Graves addressing guests at the public ceremony to celebrate the purchase of Blacka Moor.

Dear Ethel,

Here is a very green map. Buxton, with its half-moon buildings. A bridge to symbolise Bakewell. Peveril Castle, singular and proud. Matlock, Chesterfield with its unlikely, poised crooked spire, threads of roads joining them, then the names of larger settlements appearing in capitals on the side of the screen. Sheffield. Derby. Manchester. Cue an image of belching industrial chimneys.

The industry of the North Midlands and all that goes with it. Where there's muck, there's brass.

Children frolicking in the foreground. Then, the scene opening: a view of what lies beyond the town, the horizon of the Peak District. Even if you know it well, it takes your breath away, to see the contrast like that. Bus interior. Ladies in black hats.

A back garden which is common to them all. The calm centre of England.

Winding roads. A stately coach driver. Young people disembarking a train and shouldering rucksacks, wheeling bicycles. The camera lingering poignantly on a red and white platform sign reading *HOPE*. Ticket to Hope please. Return to Hope.

Serpentine drystone walls. Quiet villages. A lone man scrambling over rocks in white clothing. Blue shadows. Flat-topped stones. Sheep shearing at Ashford in the Water, the whole scene lush. Then a coach heading into bleak hill country, climbing, climbing. The artificial bodies of water at Derwent, trees shelving up and away. The ruff of water over the dam. A meadow of wild forget-me-nots. A hand plucking a flower, so easily.

Many will come again with new explorers, another day.

A coach lazily departing. Blue skies. The end.

Helen

A DETACHED HOUSE

ALTERNATIVE MATERIALS:
STUCCO
STONE COLOURED BRICKS
STONE

APPROXIMATE COST
£490 ———— £540

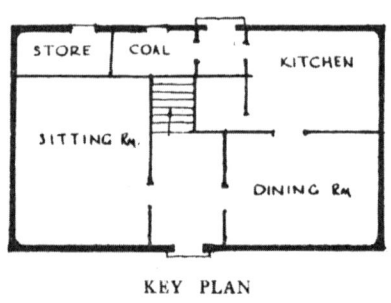

KEY PLAN

An illustration from Small Houses and Bungalows suitable for the Peak District *(1936), which showed in simplified form the house designs available from the Branch from 1935.*

Practical and pro-active campaigning: CPRE advice for better rural house designs.

The Threat to the Peak

These are great moors,
There are no walls upon them,
They sweep towards the north with scarce a field;
Strongly the rain pours,
And wind goes tearing o'er them …
(The Pride of the Peak)

Stanage Edge seen from underneath is a silent theatre. I've come here nostalgically, on the brink of a fierce storm, in the last hour of daylight, just to witness its emptiness. When I lived in Hathersage briefly, I could walk up to this spot at all the unfashionable times. It felt expectant, all the climbers departed, all the dog walkers gone home, all the pubs filling up in the nearby villages. Tonight, with the wind barrelling against the rocks, like a body battering a door, charging and charging and getting nowhere, it is eerie.

I stand with my back flat against a buttress and my arms wide and wait for the worst of it to pass. Then, recklessly, I half crawl, half scramble up a gully to the top of the edge and skitter along to the place where Robin Hood's cave waits, a calm sanctuary in the grit, an eagle's nest of a place. I wriggle my way down and traverse across until I can sneak inside, feel held and cradled by the shape of the cave, as if I'm under the protection of Stanage. From here, I can peer out and see the coming charge of the storm, bruised clouds massing in the north and inching towards my hiding place. They are so much more brooding in their approach, so much more intimidating. Anticipation is harder than endurance. When I think of Ethel, I often picture her in a spot like this, binoculars in hand, scanning for threat, for what might form on the horizon and take on a brutal shape, menacing her beloved landscape. The way she writes about Stanage in *The Pride of the Peak* is suffused with drama:

O my wide moors, what air you have, what strength
And body blows along that potent ledge,
Whereunder we will walk the whole fierce length
Even the jaggèd, sombre Stanage Edge.

It is an interesting experience to read Ethel's poetry alongside some of the factual publications she was heavily involved with, their practical structures. The covers that bind the surviving copies of *The Threat to the Peak* (published in 1931) look like summer grass, green but cracked and yellowing at the edges. It is a slim volume but a large size, just bigger than A4. It announces itself. Studying its contents gives a clear impression of what Ethel and her contemporaries would have seen as their major challenges in the early years of the Sheffield branch of CPRE's existence. Its 160 illustrations tell their own story, black and white photos, little friezes in place and time. A line of sparse trees near the Goyt Valley. A lightning fork of branches in Bretton Clough. The gnarly texture of a peat grough. Alport Castles – not a real castle at all, but a protrusion of land. Barn interiors. Rooftops. Kinder Scout, muffled by snow. It has a foreword by the eminent Cambridge historian G.M. Trevelyan where he laments the 'desecrating hand of modern man' which so damages wild places, but points optimistically to the tide of popular opinion changing and the significance of the present moment, the importance of the work being undertaken by CPRE:

> Outrages cheerfully perpetrated twenty years ago 'and nothing said' would be impossible today. Outrages possible today will be impossible twenty years hence. The future is on our side in no small degree, if we can hold the fort for another generation.

It is difficult to read such hopeful words, such references to future, in the grip of climate emergency almost a century later, when those generations march with rightful anger against the mistakes of those who came before them. Indeed, it is hard to read *The Threat to the Peak* with its emphasis on the aesthetic aspects of rural preservation in the current climate, political and actual. I have brought *The Threat to the Peak* to my stolen Stanage bunker, my weird eyrie, for exactly that reason: to read it as I brace myself against bigger, nebulous threats, ones we can't see coming, ones we pretend we haven't noticed. I want its optimism to hurt me. But I also want to be changed and heartened by Ethel's attitude, her pioneering belief in change.

Photographs by P. A. Barnes, Sheffield.

Examples of the recent and increasing defacement by advertisements in North Derbyshire, which contravene the County Council's by-laws (2*a* and *b*) under the Advertisement Regulation Acts. These by-laws forbid advertisements which "disfigure or injuriously affect views of rural scenery from a highway . . . or the amenities of any village."
(See page 21.)

WHY ARE NOT THESE EYESORES REMOVED?

A page from the 1937 CPRE annual report illustrating an effective combination of strong visuals (Phil Barnes's photographs) and Ethel's words.

It's in the preface that I hear Ethel's voice, her encyclopaedic knowledge of the Peak District. It acts as a survey of the varied landscape of the Peak District, much as her poetry does in *The Pride of the Peak*. The preface aims to transport the reader, to make them appreciate the landscape's character: central and southern regions with their limestone dales, flanked by Axe Edge to the west and Chatsworth to the east, Mam Tor and Kinder to the north; high moorlands terminating in walls of dark gritstone, like the one where I cower now – a 'jagged skyline', an 'unforgettable sight against a blue sky or against the stormy grey clouds which so often overhang'. The description of the flat-topped peat moor of Kinder Scout is perhaps the most loving though: 'fringed with black escarpments; into whose sides run deep sloughs eaten out by steeply-descending streams. The cloughs form an irregular staircase, arduous but feasible; the cascades foam and sparkle, and deep pools lie under the waterfalls.' This complex portrait is a contrast to the view beyond, separated from this idyll by low green hills of stone farms and hamlets – under a cloud of its own smoke, 'the turmoil of Sheffield'.

The tone of much of *The Threat to the Peak* is that of the moral – perhaps even religious – crusade. Throughout the carefully themed chapters, there are frequent references to God as benign creator of landscape, to the 'blasphemy' of unsympathetically rendered developments and even to Hell (capitalised in the text). The tone is sometimes gently witty or ironic however: page 43 contrasts the high tors of 'Matlock as God made it' with Matlock 'as improved by man', all gas towers and advertising hoarding. The first chapter concerns itself with 'congruous and incongruous' building, and the text dances around the photographs, incandescent at the ugly developments highlighted. A picture of suburban housing is flanked by text. 'These bungalows have pink asbestos roofs,' shrieks one side. The other concludes: 'which shatter the peaceful loveliness of their surroundings'. Chapter two adopts a similar approach to the problem of rural advertising billboards. A wonderfully incongruous example is a picture taken on the road up to the Cat and Fiddle from Buxton with a large sign announcing: 'Blackpool, 73 miles. Come now! Health, pleasure, welcome awaits you!' All is contextual, according to CPRE. Advertising has its place, but:

> There are bounds to every trade and profession, and the businessman has no more right than doctor and undertaker to injure the general wellbeing that he may better his living. The advertiser has his legitimate places … He recognises also that other places are illegitimate … During the performance of a Beethoven symphony, he is not heard shouting, 'Twenty minutes to the end, buy my pills,' 'Nineteen minutes to the end, buy my pills.' Public feeling safeguards recognised works of art, yet the countryside, so much more lovely than any work of man, is made the foil for his boastful avaricious lies, and subjected to every form of vulgarity and indignity.

It is strange to read those words in a culture where we are saturated with adverts persuading us we need to consume, where we can close our eyes and summon them, where – much of the time – we can't separate the desires of outlets and companies and institutions from our own. Yet it's also interesting to reflect that, thanks to Ethel and CPRE, we can drive or cycle to places like Stanage and escape from the bombardment of advertising imagery, find a kind of silence on roads that wind through the grit and limestone. This was not the case when Ethel was railing against intrusive billboards. The posters shown as examples look almost quaint and inoffensive compared to the assault of modern advertising, and, the text notes, these signs may not be problematic in their own right. But:

> A thing of beauty like a grand piano becomes an atrocity in a meadow, and posters which give delight in an underground railway station, give pain in a field.

Similarly, the major evil of littering is pitched as aesthetic. A contemporary text would focus on the damage to wildlife and climate, but in the early 1930s, an appeal to visual sensibility was made:

> Nature is forever changing: increasing, rotting, crumbling – working together in one great process of growth and decay. Not so litter. The sardine tin does not believe in transmigration; the moss refuses to touch the bottle, the nesting bird looks askance at the chocolate packet.

There's something quaint, almost cute about this anthropomorphism, this interest in the beliefs of the humble (but intrusive) sardine tin. Yet the effect of these juxtapositions on the reader of the 1930s might have been comparable to the effect of the film *Albatross* on me: the horror of birds ingesting plastic to feed their young.

More amusingly, the text notes: 'it is not satisfactory … to turn up a stone and be flapped at by a dirty *Daily Mail*'. Well, quite.

Chapter six directs vitriol at rural petrol stations and their ubiquity:

> To call them 'buildings' is almost an insult to that word … the medley of strident colours usual with stations is their most raucous feature.

Petrol stations have utility, CPRE acknowledges, but even where they are needed they do not have to be unsightly. A picture of a garage outside a picturesque Peak District village is captioned simply: 'Is this fair to Bakewell?' In 1928, a law had been passed by government to enable bylaws to be made controlling the building of filling stations, and *The Threat to the Peak* urges Derbyshire County Council to use these powers more stridently.

What shines through in the pages of *The Threat to the Peak* is Ethel's emphasis on the importance of education as a tool of influence and the belief held by the Sheffield branch of CPRE that many damaging decisions and behaviours were the result of ignorance. This is evident on a general scale with building work: 'lack of money is responsible for a small fraction of the evil, lack of appreciation of the country's beauty for the rest'. No wonder when 'appreciation of good building is not apparently included in the general curriculum of any school and the average citizen feels no shame of his ignorance in this respect'. The authors emphasise the 'primal need' for 'public enlightenment and particularly for sensitive appreciation of scenery'. Where wildlife and wild flowers are threatened by selfish behaviours (plucking too many flowers, stealing the eggs of birds), schools might have an active role too, encouraging children to make records of wild flowers seen rather than collecting them.

As well as education, individuals should take environmental responsibility into their own hands: 'those who witness gross acts of spoliation should explain to the offender the damage that is done'. There is an interesting mix of paternalism and individual responsibility at play in these pages. But it all connects back to Ethel's belief that access to countryside was a universal right which nobody should be denied; not a privilege for the few but a necessity for the many. In a chapter outlining industry and its relation to scenery, a strident argument is made for people having a 'natural birthright of fresh air and beauty', of which they are deprived in industrial cities. CPRE's concern is not just with the by-products of industry like smoke and pollution but with the effect on people's state of mind: lack of exposure means that 'the larger part of the population from birth onwards have no standard or knowledge of the beautiful'. Thus we create city dwellers who will 'destroy' their surroundings because they simply do not understand the natural world. There is hope, perhaps, in radicalisation; in the idea that young, active and idealistic people might be driven out of cities, propelled by their frustrations, to seek out wild corners of the countryside, to express themselves through rambler movements and outdoor adventures.

There is much that could seem problematic about the categorisations at play in *The Threat to the Peak*: the 'us' and 'them' approach to the appreciation of aesthetic natural beauty and the morality implied in this, for all the concessions made to some building work and some industry being essential to economic life. But at heart, the argument made about educating people to connect with the fabric of the world around them (indeed, not to see it as 'fabric' at all) is a wise and insightful one, perhaps a message that seems even more vital in today's apocalyptic climate. Knowledge and information as power. Appreciation as a kind of empathy. Though the reforms called for are often couched in terms of human pleasure and enjoyment, they are founded on a belief that we must collaborate, that responsibility is shared but relies on individual action.

I turn to the chapter on birds. Stately photographs of ring ouzels and red grouse, a nesting curlew, a merlin with its chicks, the speckled feathers of a golden plover. With the storm massing outside, I deny its approach and how it might shake and soak me, closing my eyes instead and thinking of all those birds populating this cave, this scant shelter. I think of Ethel Haythornthwaite's alert expression in photographs, how some might have called her bird-like. I wonder what kind of winged creature she might have been. I remember the barn owl I once glimpsed by daylight, flying from a neglected building near Bamford Edge, eerily quiet in its passage. I couldn't straightforwardly marvel at its heart-shaped face and speckled feathers against the unnervingly blue sky. I felt a knot of anxiety in my stomach: it was hunting in the daytime because it must be hungry. I'd been driving when I saw it and had stopped the car in the middle of the road. I became aware of my own menace, my own presence as an inherent threat. With ghost-strokes of its wings, the barn owl vanished between the trees of the copse. I saw it more clearly in its absence, comprehended its rarity. Perhaps Ethel would be a bird like that: gaze fixed on the trees and what they might obscure.

Dear Ethel,

I like this film, even though you aren't in it (again, again, you are nowhere to be seen). It opens at the Barrel Inn. Crowds of people, hoods up all round. What the poet Helen Dunmore called the 'privacy of rain'. Bored stone walls, dripping, aching to be more ramshackle, to be stacked in chaotic freedom. Don Paterson said:

> *I love all films that start with rain:*
> *rain, braiding a windowpane*
> *or darkening a hung-out dress*
> *or streaming down her upturned face…*

When I read that poem now, the 'her' becomes you. Most things have become you. Such is the alchemy of your presence.

On screen, men, deft on the hillside, walking fast with sticks, ant-swarming to the top of a prominent, layered rock. An elaborate cake of a rock. That's all really. The briefest glimpse of the route back down.

Little petals of water, falling with lovely constancy, setting the scene.

Helen

Gerald relaxing on Chrome Hill, with Parkhouse Hill in the background.

Vast Architecture

I cannot hold my senses, I must weep
For all the joy of love, for mate with mate:
For all the life that's quick'ning once again
For all the little lambs a-gambolling,
O heart that bursts with joy, that bursts with pain ...
                    (*The Pride of the Peak*)

In all good love stories, there is love after love, a second chance. It is as if love found and lost can never truly vanish. It broods and accumulates. It is an underground stream which reappears, under the boots, under the branches of the saplings. Little is known of Ethel's romantic engagements after the death of her beloved Henry Gallimore. It is tempting to foreground a narrative that sees her passions directed at the threatened body of the Peak District, but that would be reductive and problematic, as forced as arguments that the great writer of Scottish mountains, Nan Shepherd, imbued the Cairngorms with an eroticism she had no outlet for in life. We do know that Ethel was briefly engaged to a man during those years, the details shadowy. But in the 1930s, her life was about to change course. It would be her work through CPRE that steered her to this romantic discovery.

The second love story in Ethel's life is also a story of architecture and its resonances. Architecture, like love, is expressed through shapes, structures imbued with meaning. Mario Botta said that, 'The first gesture of an architect is to draw a perimeter ... Architecture in itself conveys this idea of limiting space. It's a limit between the finite and the infinite.' Like love, it is also founded on a degree of faith, entwined in a complex relationship with time. Both architecture and love express a kind of fundamental hope. To quote Norman Foster: 'As an architect, you design for the present, with an awareness of the past for a future which is essentially unknown.' Ethel was going to fall for an architect, someone who understood this precariousness and these certainties.

A sketch portrait of Gerald (possibly a self-portrait as his initials were G.G.).

In perhaps one of the most iconic photos of Gerald Haythornthwaite, he is reclining on a hillside in a thick jacket, right arm behind his head, windswept hair and neat moustache. He squints into a sun we can only imagine. Beside him is a large rucksack and behind him a sharp ridge juts into the day, angular and rakish. An invitation. But as representations of him go, I prefer the spare pencil sketch of his face, made around the time that he and Ethel met. There is something tentative about it, all outline and suggestion – how lines made on paper can imply the complexity and beauty of a face.

In November 1935, an advert appeared in *The Times* newspaper. It was for a technical assistant to work at the Sheffield office of CPRE. Young Gerald Haythornthwaite, in his early twenties, an architect from the outskirts of Bolton, answered the call thus:

> I am well aware of the nature of the work entailed and am deeply interested in it. If one has other than commercial interests in Architecture a national organization such as the CPRE offers more scope and opportunity for self-expression than private practice, therefore I welcome the chance to be active in this direction.

He had a glowing reference from his old professor, Reginald Cordingley, who felt that the applicant:

> has some leanings towards literary work in the field of architecture and, I think, feels that the appointment would allow him scope in such connection, without severing him from practical, professional experience. The position appears to fit his capacity admirably.

On a winter day in 1935, then, Gerald turned up in Broomhill, ready to be questioned. Jean Smart, Gerald's assistant in later life, describes him as a man who 'wanted a course rather than a career'. After graduating from Manchester University with a degree in architecture, he had initially found work at a large architectural practice in the city, a firm run by Sir Percy Worthington, but he was restless. Perhaps he always had been. His thesis (a survey of Bolton) gives some insight into his outlook and character. It is thorough, meticulous and holistic, accompanied by photographs and drawings, annotated in a sloping hand. Analysing a town plan, according to Gerald:

> necessitates a consideration of every influence that has caused its development ... this entails a detailed study of every form of social activity, the study of all the contradictions of the past in society and their eventual resolution. This demands the collaboration of every specialist in science, the doctor, the educationalist, the economist, the engineer, the architect and so on until every field of social activity has been covered.

In his thesis, Gerald comes across as ambitious and self-possessed, but also aware of the limitations of his knowledge. In the introduction he also concedes that his analysis is just a 'unit' in a bigger picture, 'a unit which must be full of faults and ignorance where ever [sic] it passes beyond the field of the author's specialized knowledge and common sense'. He describes his contribution as both 'spasmodic' and 'approximate'.

Gerald was the son of a man who was a partner in a Bolton printing firm, but who amassed huge debts and was credited with little business sense by those who knew him. He had a brother, Noel, whose sudden death at the age of eight was a source of profound and irreconcilable disagreement between his parents. His mother needed his father to be present to sign for Noel to have an operation for peritonitis, an inflammation of thin tissue inside the abdomen, which can become fatal if left untreated. The father could not be found – reportedly off at the golf course. Noel died. This must have introduced an instability to the early life of Gerald and his sister Jean. Gerald was reportedly distant from his biological family for much of his life. His Aunt Annie was a source of constant stability for him: it was she who paid for his education at Manchester University and offered him some degree of financial aid through formative points of his life. This was the young man – recently qualified, slightly rootless – who turned up in suburban Sheffield in 1935, keen to prove himself.

What Ethel responded to, no doubt, was Gerald's love of the countryside and interest in the structures that we might place in and around it. He described his early childhood in an interview with Fiona Reynolds in 1988, the legacy of his time at Bolton School and the influence of Bill Brooks, the scoutmaster:

> We used to go onto the Belmont Moors almost every weekend for a weekend camp and we used to go to the Lakes and Wales and also abroad ... the first national park that I ever saw was the Ordesa National Park in Spain. He took us up the Ordesa Valley to the Brèche de Roland and up a 100-foot piece of sandstone with a 2,000-foot drop below us – he must have been a very brave man. He did actually bring us all out of that alive.

Bill's influence extended to architecture as well:

> He used to, wherever we went, have a look at the notable buildings. Jumièges, we had to go there and look at the ruin, and in [Caen] we went to have a look at the Abbaye aux Dames and so forth and so I got a very wide interest in the countryside then and also its buildings, and this stayed with me.

For Gerald, architecture was about context: buildings understood through their surroundings. Though it wasn't published until 1988, he might have agreed with much of Gaston Bachelard's philosophy in *The Poetics of Space*:

> Rilke wrote: 'These trees are magnificent, but even more magnificent is the sublime and moving space between them, as though with their growth it too increased.'

Ethel, twenty years his senior, must have made a formidable impression on Gerald too. His age was an immediate source of speculation. They entered into correspondence both before and after his interview, with Ethel tentatively testing the waters, challenging his commitment to the organisation:

> Will you tell me your age, please? If you took this place would you be prepared to stay not less than two or three years?

We hardly blink at narratives of older men in positions of power forming relationships with women decades their junior. We seldom revel in stories where the gender dynamic is reversed and where the woman is senior, powerful and established, more experienced in relationships. When CPRE decided to appoint young Gerald Haythornthwaite, Ethel remarked pointedly in her letter to him:

> I might say the standard of lettering and draughtsmanship shown in the drawings you left here is not quite up to our previous standard.

Lynn Crowe, emeritus professor of environmental management at Sheffield Hallam University, who worked as Gerald's assistant in the 1980s, describes Gerald as being very visual, interested in photographs and mapping what change might actually look like – the architect's instinct for visualising detail. As well as a faith in the restorative powers of the countryside, Ethel and Gerald shared a love of poetry and literature, as she and Henry had done. It is tempting to fancifully recreate the early days of their secret, blossoming romance, imagining long walks through limestone, languid picnics on the banks of rivers, sheltering under each other's coats in summer thunder, reading to each other on the banks of the Porter, angling their bodies towards home. A blanket in summer, their legs braided over one another as they sat and each studied a book, islands touching. But there is a prurience in this, an unhealthy curiosity. And love is like other people's dreams – something we can stray to the outskirts of and never wholly enter.

Ethel and Gerald were married in December 1937 – some two years after their first meeting – at Sheffield Register Office. There was nobody present at the ceremony. Gerald's mother was rumoured to be unhappy about the age difference between the couple. Similarly, Ethel's sister Gertie found their marriage difficult to accept, and Gerald and Gertie's relationship remained strained for much of their lives, for all they shared a fierce affection for Ethel and an unwavering instinct to support her. Ethel's brother, Alan, gave the newly-weds a Rolls-Royce as a wedding present. Others quickly convinced Gerald that the model was too dangerous and he sold it for a 1927 Rolls Tourer, which would reportedly stay with the family until 1957. As Gerald would reflect later in conversation with Fiona Reynolds, they entwined their fates, and forged a partnership that would last a lifetime:

> I married my boss. In 1937, Ethel Gallimore became Ethel Haythornthwaite and without question her influence was number one. I'm not saying that because I married her, or perhaps I married her because of that, I don't know, but she not only achieved a good deal in the way of purchases like Longshaw but she managed to persuade a number of very hard-headed businessmen to put their capital into the purchase of land in the national park.

The phrase 'perhaps I married her because of that' seems glib, but perhaps what he meant was that part of his obvious attraction to Ethel was her drive and commitment, her integrity and her ability to get things done. He was evidently impressed by her. In interviews with Gerald, we learn frustratingly little of Ethel's character beyond a list of her achievements – things that are recorded by other sources. Even in these accounts by someone married to her, she remains somehow enigmatic, her personality inferred from the things she did, from her work. But it is touching that Gerald considered his wife 'number one' in the list of influential figures who were behind the influence of CPRE.

In the weeks after their marriage, the pair honeymooned in Swaledale, Yorkshire. At the heart of Swaledale, the River Swale, one of the fastest-rising flood rivers in England, flows through hay meadows, surrounded by miles of drystone walls and dotted with carefully preserved stone field barns. In summer, it is dense with unruly wild flowers, awash with colour. One of the most northerly of the dales, it is renowned for feeling 'wild' and 'unspoiled'. Many of the villages and tiny hamlets – such as Gunnerside (from 'Gunnar's saetr') – still carry the names given to them by Viking farmers who settled there over a thousand years ago. This must have been inspirational to Gerald and Ethel, troubled as they were by the incursions into the Peak District.

On their return, the couple moved to nearby Stumperlowe Crescent Road, but the billiard room at Endcliffe Vale House continued to be CPRE headquarters. Now that they were married, the serving chairperson of CPRE decided to split their roles up, sending Gerald to work in the architecture department at Sheffield town hall. Before Gerald's role at CPRE, Ethel had employed another young architect called John Worsnip, whose work was concerned with regulating the kind of housing which could be built in the Peak District. Gerald would later recall that Worsnip:

> set up a portfolio of designs for builders to buy and for which they paid £2 for a working set of drawings. He also designed a booklet, the first, I think, that came out in this country. It was called *Housing in the Peak [District]* and this had a very good issue indeed. I forget how many copies were sold but it was a great number and this set up the whole process of site selection, materials selection and adequate designs and so forth, so I was able to take on from that as soon as he'd gone. I had to go out and harangue builders and climb up onto ridges and you know, argue with them about what they were doing.

The foreword to *Housing in the Peak District* (sold for one shilling) was written by E. Guy Dawber (past president of the Royal Institute of British Architects and then chairman of the Council for the Preservation of Rural England). Its tone is damning, branding many constructions 'ugly', 'pretentious', 'deplorable' and 'badly built', describing a landscape 'desecrated' by development. There is a distinct implication of immorality on the part of those deemed responsible:

> The beauty of our English countryside is daily being disfigured, not only by the thoughtlessness of speculative builders, but also through the apathy and indifference of the public ... At present the trouble is that our senses for so long have been blunted by this sort of thing, and our eyes so accustomed to these buildings, that many are by no means convinced even of the necessity or desirability of any sort of change.

The answer, according to Dawber, lay not in planning legislation (difficult to implement) but in education – an ethos which Ethel very much shared:

Had we taught, fifty years ago, the people of this country, adults and children in our elementary, secondary and public schools and universities, the value of our beautiful countryside, its trees and scenery, its villages, churches and old buildings, and objects of historic interest – civic pride in fact – we should not to-day be suffering from this spate of ugliness that is overwhelming the whole country.

The language is often that of the epidemic, or even pandemic: pristine countryside swamped by deplorable developments. It is the language of fear. But the proposed solution was much more measured and took account of the fact that new houses, new buildings are often essential to the population. The aim of *Housing in the Peak District* was to set out 'in a clear and convincing manner' what might be done to integrate new developments with their setting, in terms of materials, aspect, design and layout.

Nonetheless, the contents of the book are delightfully outraged and judgemental in tone. The pages are filled with black and white photographs taken by Phil Barnes with commentary. Examples of good practice are given as well as instances of disaster. An image of a gritstone cottage sits below a photograph of Stanage Edge: 'Note: walls and roof of local stone; long narrow plan; simplicity and strength.' Often, the desirable housing is imbued with human characteristics. Roofs at Tissington are considered to possess 'dignity' or even 'modesty'. In Parwich, the 'delightful effect of a continuous line of buildings facing the village green' is praised. Wrath is saved for those buildings which display uneven lines, 'disorder and vulgarity'. In a photo of suburban Sheffield, individuality is condemned: 'each house strives to be different from its neighbours and the result is chaos. Note the unfortunate jagged roof line.' Much effort is given to distinguishing between 'pleasant' and 'unpleasant' bungalows, particularly in suburbia. Startlingly, one example is described as 'smug', a strange anthropomorphism. Shoddy builders come under fire as well:

> Owing to its cheapness and efficiency, slate has been widely employed by incompetent builders and this has led to a prejudice against the material which is unfounded. In skilled hands slate can be used with fine effect.

But the purpose of the booklet is also to instruct and advise, and there seems to have been an attempt to establish rules and principles for good design, from features like windows and doors, to aspect, layout and grouping. In a section on suitable design, the writer notes:

> It is much easier to design a dignified symmetrical building than an unsymmetrical one ... houses should never be made irregular just to obtain a 'picturesque' or pretty effect. It is true that many of the old buildings are quaintly irregular, but this has been brought about by practical considerations ... where there is no practical reason for them, irregularity and 'quaintness' merely look absurd.

This is the legacy that Gerald inherited, an outlook with which he would have been in sympathy. His passion for buildings which would not intrude on the landscape is perhaps best expressed in a piece he published in *The Countryman* in 1964:

> A building and the details of its construction grow taut and sing like a tightly drawn string when no more and no less materials are used than are needed for each part to do its job.

He goes on to illustrate this with the example of stone dressings round window openings, rhapsodising about materials:

> Long before we started to calculate the strength of materials, our forefathers had acquired by experience a precise knowledge of the depth and thickness of stone needed for the lintel to bear the weight of the walls ... they gave to these details proportions which satisfy the eye. Immature mathematics and physics entered in about the middle of the nineteenth century and let loose a flood of coarse, over-weighted, over-secure structural members which gave no pleasure.

He concludes his article tellingly with the bracketed words, 'To be continued'.

Ethel and Gerald's work together over the decades that followed would establish them as a formidable partnership. Those who knew them, like Jean Smart, described them as a pair of contrasts. Ethel was frugal: she never bought paper clips, seldom switched on lights. The only exception was her health: she would travel to London's prestigious Harley Street for appointments. Gerald, perhaps in the shadow of his father, was more extravagant by nature. He was also, perhaps, slightly more reckless. His papers reveal a delightfully formal caution from Sheffield police in February 1946 for driving without working lights on Pitt Street, or rather, as they put it, causing a vehicle 'to be on a road during the hours of darkness without carrying two lamps, each shewing to the front a white light, visible from a reasonable distance, and a lamp shewing to the rear a red light visible from a reasonable distance … contrary to the Road Transport Lighting Act 1927, Section 1.' The chief constable added:

> No further action will be taken in this case, but I am to inform you that if you are reported again it may be necessary to take proceedings against you in respect of the latter case.

A small slap on the wrist for carelessness. In contrast to Ethel's financial savvy, he bought sharp suits from Savile Row, had his shirts tailor-made on Jermyn Street and sent all of his dry cleaning to London. Poignantly, this would only be reversed after Ethel's death where, in old age, Gerald sought to emulate her habits.

Not long after the early days of their marriage and the start of their work together, war once more threatened Ethel's happiness. Gerald was in the Territorial Army and in 1939 was called up to fight. The trauma for Ethel must have been acute, still-raw memories of losing Henry to battle. They wrote to each other as often as possible. In a letter to her lover, Ethel wrote bleakly:

> You are the poignant thing in my mind. How I wish you could be spared this undeserved thing.

Through that tense time, Ethel moved back into Endcliffe Vale House and threw herself into the service of the countryside once more. As she wrote to her friend John Batton:

> While most healthy women can do some kind of emergency work, there are only such a limited number who see what rural England means to the English and therefore would work to save it.

Ethel refused to be consumed by despondency during this uncertain and frightening time. She argued that her work was more important than ever during this time and that CPRE and all its branches should strive to hold on, despite the chaos around them. The alternative was unthinkable, for if they could not, 'much more of England's beauty will be lost for those who return after the war, or for those who must carry on the country even over our dead bodies. I never thought myself of letting go till we really must. I believe our aims are too profoundly important for that.'

Through the war, Gerald became a lieutenant colonel. He served in London, Algiers and Norway, but he would return safely to Ethel in 1945. It must have felt like their first meeting all over again, that office in the 1930s, the keen, alert architecture graduate and the reserved honorary secretary of the Sheffield branch of CPRE, waiting coolly to be impressed by him.

Ethel and Gerald (now Lt Col. Haythornthwaite) relaxing in the grounds of Endcliffe Vale House, during the war years.

Dear Ethel,

All morning, through *The Pride of the Peak*, through the taut stanzas of your poem, you have been teaching me new words:

Blikken: to shine
Cruddle: to cower, bend down
Glizzen: to sparkle, shine

You seem preoccupied with shining. I don't blame you. The landscape after rain, the beauty of windowpanes touched by a storm.
I also love your words for claggy ground and weather:

Roky: cloudy, foggy
Sanky: boggy, spongy
Slape: slippery

Derwent Edge in autumn, the spongy, wobbly ground. Perhaps a hare startling in the distance. It is all so wholly Derbyshire. I did not know that black mud was called 'soar' or that 'scaddle' means timid. I was unfamiliar with the word 'slome' which means to wander aimlessly. I had no idea that someone wan or pale could be described as 'watchet'. Best of all perhaps is 'weather-breeder', a fine warm day in autumn or winter. Oh, for such days!
I have been in the archive again, searching. And at last, here you are. The only known film footage of Ethel, Mrs E.M.B. Gallimore. I am fidgety with excitement. September 1936 (the date underlined). Surprise View, Derbyshire, becomes the property of the National Trust. I know this place so well, love how it reveals itself to anyone who wants to see.
Watch. A striking diagonal of people in coats, stretching up the hillside. Poised, intent, barely a movement. Then a tall, slender woman in a hat, smiling and shaking hands. Is this you, Ethel? Why am I looking for you everywhere? Then, a makeshift stage, four men and there, second from the left, a woman in dark clothing, sensible heeled shoes, hat pulled down.

There you are. At last. You have a sheaf of papers on your lap – the deeds – and you briskly adjust the hem of your jacket, smoothing it. Then, in a lovely, efficient movement, you bend and reach to retrieve a slip of paper from the stage floor and place it on the table of the man speaking. Unobtrusive. I wish you had made more of a show of your usefulness. You seem so busy and quiet, always rummaging or adjusting something. After the men have spoken, it's your moment. You stand. You relinquish the deeds. Your smile is wide as you sit down. And that's all. I wish they had let you speak properly. I wish they had put you at the centre of the stage.

 Helen

A cartoon used for CPRE's 1930s green belt campaign.

The Belt

Boldly the boulders o'er the valley stand,
And lift their heads against the lofty air;
Their jutting crags command the lower land
Like couchant dragons looking from their lair.
(*The Pride of the Peak*)

Where does Sheffield as I know it end? The notion of a green belt feels almost enchanted, like one of those children's books where a tree reveals a hidden door, or a wardrobe is porous, or a knife cuts a gleeful window in the air. To find the edges of the city as Ethel would have experienced them, I have to go above it and below. In her essay collection *Findings*, Kathleen Jamie chastises us for not looking upwards enough, not studying the tops of buildings and cities. She describes a transformative moment in Edinburgh:

> I was crossing Charlotte Square ... I happened to look up and, between chimney stacks and cupolas, saw this beautiful brass comet, a shining ball towing a deeply forked tail. Maybe I don't look upward enough ... before the comet, I'd never wondered what the city raises ... what its domes and spires offer to the winds.

The same can be true of walking. We stare at the ground and miss the heights of things, the tips of trees, the uppermost branches. I am setting out uphill, cycling through Crookes and Crosspool, thinking of John Donne:

Licence my roving hands, and let them go,
Before, behind, between, above, below

I'm imagining those sensual words, addressed to a lover, transformed into an instruction to the feet, the body in landscape. License my roving steps.

I need to be above this stretch of open land, in front of it and overshadowed by it, pressed by its edges.

Today, I want to climb. I also want to dart under the surface of the city, to be a stitch, just for a moment. So I go to Redmires, where I can do both. I cycle to the place where the road runs out and abandon my bike, trusting that nobody here will steal it. If I can't have faith in that, what can I have faith in? It's an off-grey day anyway, and there's nobody to rob me except grouse (heard but not seen) and perhaps, I fancy, a curlew. I imagine a curlew atop a bicycle, stately, using its curved beak for balance. I strike off from the track to the left and answer the call of water, the path winding round to a little shore. I once swam here when the light was breaking, 5 a.m., chill and misty. Everything was under a sheet until suddenly it wasn't: some unseen hand whisked the mist away and I was left with glassy water and the intent stare of the sun.

I am shedding layers. I am wading in. The mud sucks at your toes here, feels almost inviting, cushioned. There are ducks bumbling around by the bank, reprimanding each other, diving theatrically. I walk out until I am up to my knees, then my waist. I stop and watch the ripples that arch out from me, seeking. What do I want from this body of water? What does it want from me? Perhaps it wants me to leave it alone. Sheffield is full of 'wild' swimmers, cheerful on Sundays with their dryrobes and cameras. I imagine the ripples telling me to *go home, go home, go home*. But I am obstinate and – by my human nature – arrogant, so I trust myself to the water anyway and plunge in, up to my neck, then duck my head under and come up spluttering.

Later I will dry off and follow the path along to Stanage Pole and from there to the edge where I can peer down like a child who wants to be so much taller. Bracken. The spectre of the dark woods. The boulders that preoccupy climbers, fascinated by their small puzzles which feel like big puzzles.

'I am always obsessed by one place or another,' says M. John Harrison in his delightfully slippery anti-memoir *Wish I Was Here*. Trying to describe a specific part of Wales ('the enchanted hinterland' between the A496 road and the Rhinogydd) he says:

> There's a real sense, in this landscape, of haunting, but rarely by anything specific. Yes the trace of use, but the moment you try to imagine by whom, or for what, or begin to believe you might 'bring it to life', it slips quietly back into the twilight downslope, the

wind-contorted tree. Every site is very calm, despite the things it must have seen. Even to say that is to say too much ... Where everything you can say is either an understatement or an overstatement, a liberalisation or a fiction, it's not your place to say anything.

I stand on the edge. I try to keep my mouth shut for once. I try to keep my mind quiet, but it is full of surroundings, Sheffield's borders.

※

Describing her early apprehension of Sheffield, Ethel once said:

> My childhood impressions of the city were – a gloomy noisy shapeless phenomenon: but outside the city – there one began to live. To escape into the clean air, the gradual return to nature; with these came satisfaction and peace ... Along with this came the sickening realisation, as the ugly suburbs straggled out and the farms disappeared, that it was all going. But a helpless uneasiness may be replaced by action, and now some who comprehended the significance of Sheffield's surroundings to her citizens, spend a large part of their lives trying to save them.

I'm interested by Ethel's depiction here of Sheffield as female. The somewhat cloying image of landscape as the female body, to be protected but also conquered, or at the very least charted. The attempt to secure a green belt for Sheffield – a big preoccupation for CPRE over decades – could be seen as an attempt to enforce shape, to cinch the city's waist; so much of the language from the time feels problematic to a modern audience, but the intent was to preserve and protect, to safeguard, to cherish.

In *The Story of Sheffield's Green Belt and a Guide to its Future* published by CPRE in 1984, the purposes of a green belt are neatly summarised:

1. To prevent the sprawl of towns which are already far too big for the comfort or pleasure of the citizens.
2. To provide the townsman with the opportunity to escape from the noise, congestion and strain of city life and to seek refreshment in the countryside.

The image of a townsman seeking refreshment conjures up visions of bowler-hatted executives spilling their beer outside the Norfolk Arms.

And the idea of a town too big for the 'pleasure' of its citizens might warrant some unpicking. But CPRE's statement of purpose declared the urgency of protecting the area's river valleys which 'penetrate as green wedges deeply into the built-up areas of the city, providing ready and attractive access to the open countryside', a countryside considered a 'special asset', absent from the environs of most industrial cities.

In 1936, a speculative builder bought eighty-four acres on the north side of Hathersage Road and nine acres opposite the Dore Moor Inn. The plan was to build almost a thousand new houses. Ethel went to consult with her influential friend Alderman Marshall, who rallied in outrage, noting that it was not just this area they had a responsibility to: 'we must save them all,' he famously said. After successful campaigning by Ethel and others – notably Marshall – the Corporation of Sheffield eventually paid the builder £22,000 in compensation (with CPRE offering to contribute £3,000 if needed) to stop the housing development taking place. It would have been keen to avoid having to pay such large compensatory sums in future, so perhaps that made officials more than usually receptive to Ethel's view that they should 'fix some limit as to where the town should end and the country begin'. Ethel addressed the Highways and Planning Committee, expressing a hope that the Whirlow area could be permanently saved as a kind of space where no building other than agricultural would be allowed and then consider expanding that to secure a larger, permanent green belt area. She concluded her address:

> The possession of such fine country at its doors has always been our City's greatest pride: the loss of it would be its greatest catastrophe.

In her 1954 lantern talk reflecting on the eventual demarcation of the green belt, Ethel reflected on the longevity of the campaign. 'It took seven years to get the Council to take action on our report and it was not until 1933 that the Sheffield Bylaws prohibiting disfigurement by advertisement in rural areas were adopted.'

Looking back on her intervention to save the area between Totley and Owler Bar, and her offer to buy it, she mused:

> In the north you know, we never believe folks are genuine till their pockets are touched.

Summarising the outcome, she highlighted the importance of those involved seeing the landscape:

> A special meeting of councillors was arranged. A fleet of taxis proceeded to Owler Bar. They looked on the threatened upland. They said 'this shall not be spoiled'. The plans went to blazes and my pocket was saved – til the next emergency.

Alderman Marshall reinforced Ethel's conviction at every turn, exerting pressure on the Highways and Planning Committee. In her lantern talk, Ethel would give thanks to him, noting, 'he could be relied on not only to be enthusiastic but firm. He did not give way and neither did we.' At an executive meeting in 1936, Marshall stated that he was taking a deep personal interest in securing a green belt on all sides of the city. In 1937, CPRE was asked to submit a map of where it felt a green belt should be.

Ethel and Gerald carried out the surveying work together, mapping the moors on all the fringes of the city and visiting areas that overlapped with other local authorities. Their recommendations were submitted on 1 February and came under several headings. First, they had identified areas they felt should be preserved as green belt. The biggest of these was a vast moorland and upland pasture area taking in parts of Dore and Totley, Ringinglow, Redmires, Wyming Brook, the Porter and Rivelin valleys, and Burbage and Houndkirk – areas that swarm with fell runners today on wind-scoured Sundays, recognised as challenging terrain. To this, they added Beeley Wood, Birley Edge and strips of farmland on the borders with Derbyshire. They even included parts of the east and north-east, already subject to much industrial development: Tinsley Park golf course and High Hazels Park were notable, in the area where the iconic Tinsley cooling towers once stood, known today as the side of town that houses the eerie green domes of Meadowhall shopping centre. Ethel would refer to this part of Sheffield as 'that long-suffering region'.

Having sketched out these parameters, Ethel and Gerald moved on to the issue of how areas included as green belt should be treated. The headline was that they must be 'strictly rural', with building only allowed for limited agricultural purposes. In some locations, they felt that playing fields would be a suitable use for the land. Where building was necessary, this should be sympathetically done, with local stone used and advice taken from CPRE-approved architects. They also emphasised the importance of getting

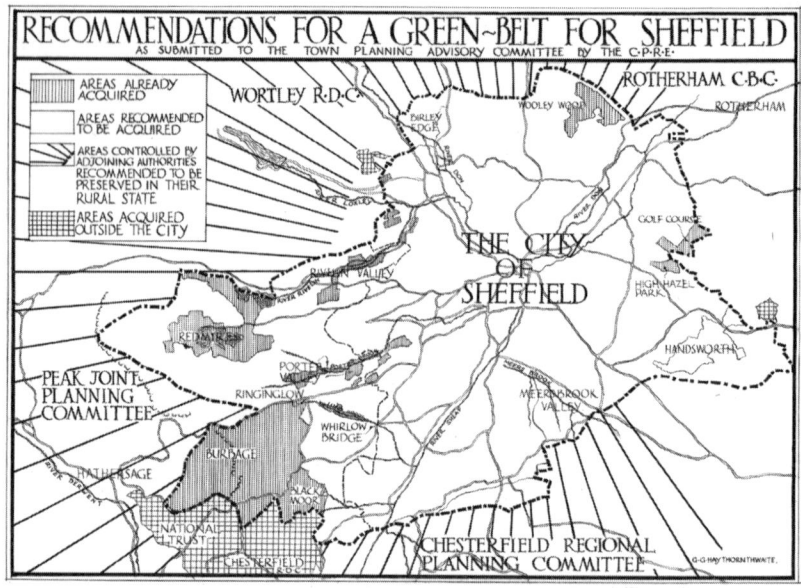

Gerald's hand-drawn plan detailing CPRE's proposals for a Sheffield green belt.

neighbouring local authorities to cooperate: some areas to the north of Sheffield (like Loxley and Ecclesfield) were governed by West Riding County Council. To the south, the Chesterfield Regional Planning Committee had responsibilities for areas close to Coal Aston, Mosborough and Eckington.

All of these plans were approved by the corporation by a small majority in 1938. But this was only the first victory in a long war of attrition, a steady, slow change, like water over stones. And it would be interrupted by the advent of the Second World War. Members of the public considered the green belt an established fact, but Ethel was suspicious, watchful, eager to remind the corporation to honour its commitments. After all, it was still provisional in the sense that it had no legal protection. And her staunch ally, Alderman Marshall, was on the verge of leaving the corporation. Some of Ethel's worst fears were confirmed when the government ordered the construction of a war factory near Middlewood Road, north of the River Don. Ethel was of the firm conviction that an alternative site could have been found. The corporation had – in the eyes of CPRE – failed to properly consult, using the war as a distraction. Even during a testing personal time for Ethel, with Gerald away and her memory of Henry Gallimore's death awakened, she remained focused, attentive, refusing to let her defence of the green belt slip.

The aftermath of war brought further challenges. In 1951, there was population pressure in Sheffield after slum clearances. The corporation began to enviously eye the green open spaces within their own belt and those in the catchment areas of neighbouring counties too. They promoted an extension bill to take 1,400 acres of Derbyshire land and 6,490 acres from the West Riding and, when this failed, suggested building on 400 acres in the Meersbrook, Rivelin and Sheaf valleys. Ethel and Gerald (now Lieutenant Colonel Haythornthwaite) led the argument against the scheme, arguing that there was a pressing need to rebuild blitzed and cleared areas close to the centre of Sheffield and reminding the corporation that there was land available to develop at Handsworth, Greenhill, Arbourthorne, Hackenthorpe and Brincliffe, all outside the provisional green belt. Their objections were supported by a petition with well over 6,000 signatures from members of the public. But success was partial: some areas of Meersbrook and Rivelin were allowed to be purchased and built on, and there was approval for building huge tower blocks at Gleadless; today they sit beside the huge expanse of woodland. I imagine the flats and trees watching each other uneasily, each briefly aspiring to the condition of the other.

It is important to note that Ethel and her allies were not naively opposed to the development of new housing per se. It would be easy for people of their social privilege to remain comfortably insulated, distanced from the problems of accessing affordable and suitable living spaces (and indeed, Ethel's manner of describing some of the industrial parts of the city in the north-east could seem a little condescending). They accepted that changes were necessary, that new housing was necessary. But they rejected the idea that this had to continue inexorably outwards into areas of outstanding natural beauty. It stemmed, perhaps, from Ethel and Gerald's belief that access to green space was a fundamental human right, a source of spiritual enlightenment and intellectual improvement. In some ways, there's something a little paternalistic about this, a sense of the middle and upper classes knowing best, or championing a kind of virtue. But it came from a kind of generosity, from Ethel wanting others to have the same transformative experience of countryside that she had.

A key suggestion CPRE made with regard to housing was that there was land towards North East Derbyshire which could be used for building without impinging on the green belt. In 1967, approval was given to extend the Sheffield city boundaries to incorporate 5,050 acres of Derbyshire land, including the villages of Mosborough and Beighton. There was potential for this area to accommodate an overspill of 40,000 people. The Mosborough area is a place I used to mooch around as a child, because my dad was an

English teacher in the secondary school there. I remember new estates shoulder to shoulder with old cottages, the large pub and the presence of fields, the nearness of Rother Valley Country Park with its flat water and spooky tunnel bridges. It had the character of a Nottinghamshire mining village, and my dad always talked about reading D.H. Lawrence to his students and them finding some of it relatable. I always felt a kinship with Mosborough as someone who lived in North East Derbyshire: it was a gateway to Sheffield. Ethel had always insisted it was the place to build.

When I think about what a belt really is, I think of something flexible as well as durable. I think of the edges of Sheffield adapting to an imaginary shape, widening and waning. In 1955, MP Duncan Sandys, the Minister of Housing and Local Government, issued a circular to planning authorities which called for a check on unrestricted housing sprawl across the country. A tightening of the belt. Local authorities were invited to submit boundary plans. The green belt plan for Sheffield finally became operative in December 1983, nearly half a century after CPRE first began campaigning for it. An inspector appointed by the Secretary of State for the Environment noted the special circumstances for Sheffield, which justified its green belt being 'tightened' more than elsewhere:

> Foremost among the reasons for having the green belt tightly drawn is the remarkable quality of the landscape on all sides of the city but the east. It is a landscape of bold relief with spurs of high land separating valleys which are often deep and which provide natural 'green wedges' into the built up area. (Mr D.F. Harris, 1982)

It is because of the green belt legislation that I can wander the moorland beyond Redmires, joining up vast networks of paths. I can lose elevation and take the track by Wyming Brook, curving down to meet the water. In winter here, the trees are indelible. It is thanks to Ethel's insistence that I can explore the Trans Pennine Trail out from Woodhouse and towards the part of North East Derbyshire where I spent most of my childhood, running through Shirebrook, startled by the skittish movements of a stoat or weasel – some tiny and unlikely thing – across the leaves in front.

I am going into the water again. I've done my circuit and I'm back for another immersion. Sinking into Redmires always stirs up mixed feelings, silty, murky feelings that dissolve with the action of swimming, the clarity of cool water. So much of outdoor swimming in an area like this is predicated on a nebulous kind of trespass, venturing into reservoirs and ponds where access is not officially condoned. I like the subversiveness of it; I think of Norman MacCaig, the great Scottish poet, reflecting on his love of Assynt, the remote and endless horizons of the North West Highlands:

Who owns this landscape? –
The millionaire who bought it or
the poacher staggering downhill in the early morning
with a deer on his back?

Who possesses this landscape? –
The man who bought it or
I who am possessed by it?

Why should we not climb fences? Why should we not go where our feet take us? Why should we not plunge in? But, on the other hand, I resist the kind of glib entitlement that can accompany those kinds of movements through space and place. Why should I get in the water just because I can? Why am I not content to look at it? I hate the detritus around places like Stanage in summer. I am terrified by the wildfires that rage across parched moorlands, started by careless fires or cigarettes. I distrust the human impulse to leave traces, even as I made these brash marks across the page with my clattering keys, my clumsy typing. I do know that I like to feel the way the water touches me, finds out my weaknesses, how when I emerge again I feel that I am being spat out, that I've reached the edge of my familiar landscape and somehow ducked under it, tried to be a stitch but come back unstitched, undone, ready to begin the daily business of sense-making all over again.

Dear Ethel,

I'm studying your back and the outline of your face as you glance over your left shoulder. It feels almost prurient. You're on the back of your beloved horse, Bracken, on an elevated track above bordered fields, your route hugging a drystone wall. Bracken is dark with a luxuriant, long tail. I love how horses look as if they're wearing flares. You're dressed in a light-coloured trench coat, billowing at the arms, the hood slightly crumpled behind you. You wear no helmet and your short hair is messy. I wonder if you're setting off or about to turn for home.

There is something whippet-like about you, your shape and your strength. Lithe and capable. Am I allowed to say I like your hairstyle? It is short and practical; there's something decisive about it. It protrudes wilfully from under hats and helmets, your angular face cupped.

I tried to ride a horse yesterday, imagining your trips with Bracken around the Peak District boundary, gentle hoofprints in soft ground. I am no horsewoman. I struggled my way on to the creature's flanks, undignified, and sudden movements spooked me. But I loved the rolling, shambling rhythm of riding. I loved the way my horse kept pausing to have opportunistic snacks: low-hanging branches and protruding ferns. I was told she was middle-aged and lazy, and I felt an instant affinity to her, how she takes her pleasure where she can. The landscape looks and feels different on horseback. Instead of feeling it through your feet, you feel it through the rolling movement of the horse, the uneven ground, the camber. I imagined you, upright and confident with Bracken, plotting the Peak District boundary.

Helen

AREA OF PROPOSED NATIONAL PARK
as recommended by The Peak District National Park Joint Committee

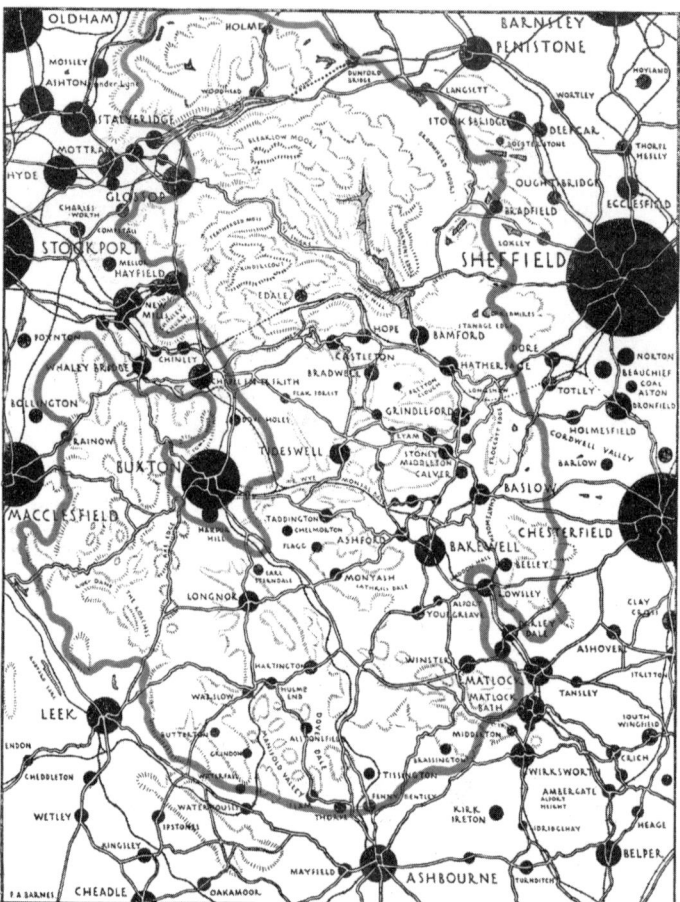

The National Trust already owns 4,350 acres in the area and has, in addition, protection over 3,100 acres.

The plan of the proposed area to be designated as national park – as drawn by Phil Barnes – reproduced in *The Peak District: A National Park* (1944).

A National Park

Up to this world, all bounding, bright and free,
Where the Ridge leaps in strength, and Mam Tor stands
A fort among the hills and scarce a tree
Crouches upon the green and rolling lands.
(*The Pride of the Peak*)

In his foreword to Melvyn Jones's meticulous history of the Sheffield branch of CPRE, Sir Chris Bonington observes:

> Whatever else is forgotten, the Branch will go down in history as a major force in environmental conservation because of the achievement of its two 'grand purposes': the designation of a national park in the Peak District and the creation of a permanent Sheffield Green Belt.

Today, it seems difficult to imagine the UK without its demarcated national parks. One might almost think they've been part of life forever, particularly in Sheffield where the park is almost deemed part of 'the outdoor city'. Ethel's role in the struggle to establish the Peak District as a pioneering example of how a national park might benefit the population is perhaps one of her better-known achievements.

On 22 March 2019, I gathered with hundreds of others in the car park at Castleton on an inauspicious, strangely muggy day. I strapped my four-month-old son to my chest in a sling, cosy in his blue padded suit. Then I followed the crocodile of strangers up the road towards Mam Tor, walking hesitantly; this would be the furthest I'd attempted carrying him. Acquaintances and old friends talked to me, nodded to the baby, but the friendliest reaction by far came from Yvonne Witter of Peak District Mosaic, an organisation whose aim is to create (and sustain) engagement between the Peak Park and new audiences, including black, Asian and minority ethnic communities. Yvonne and her colleagues asked me questions about my little one and my love of Derbyshire and described recent trips they'd organised or been part of.

We were there to mark the anniversary of the Peak District National Park, and I was struck by what a diverse group we were (at least, at a glance – a range of genders, ages and ethnicities, though I was making that judgement based only on appearances). The mood was jubilant, despite the sun's resolute refusal to appear. I walked alongside park rangers, photographers, CPRE members and trustees. Alfie, I'm convinced, was the youngest participant on the walk and many remarked that he had the easiest job, snoozing in his snug carrier while I sweated in the humidity, the gradient seeming more punishing than it should have done.

We took the path to the Great Ridge and massed there, enjoying the views towards Edale on one side and Hope and Castleton on the other. My son wriggled slightly, but mostly he slept. I became anxious about getting down before he woke and set off alone down the steep slope. A selfie I took that day shows me with a crossroads sign behind me, signposting Hollins Cross and Mam Tor, Back Tor and Lose Hill.

When did the seeds of the proposal for a national park in the Peak District begin to grow? It was such a lengthy process it's hard to be definitive. As early as 1937, it had been decided that the Sheffield branch of CPRE should map out local areas which would be suitable for inclusion. But the Manchester Ramblers' Federation had already been vocal on the issue in 1930, suggesting it should be an area of 205 square miles encompassing northern gritstone moorlands and including picturesque Dovedale too.

It is impossible to discuss the Manchester Ramblers without lingering on the influence of G.H.B. Ward, founder of the Sheffield Clarion Ramblers in 1900 and no relation to Ethel, despite their shared name. In fact, it seems remarkable to have considered her life thus far without mentioning his influence.

Ward and the Clarion Ramblers were the working-class counterpart to Ethel's middle-class bartering. Rather than attending university as Ethel did, Ward (known as Bert) lost his mother at the age of nine and left school at twelve or thirteen. One of his early crowning achievements was being kicked out of the church where he was working as a Sunday school teacher because of his vocal socialism. An active trade unionist and secretary of the local Labour Representation Committee, he founded the Clarion Ramblers when he was just twenty-four, the idea spawned during a twenty-mile hike from Jacob's Ladder in Edale to Hayfield, then via William Clough, Ashop Clough and Hope.

As founder of the Clarion Ramblers, Ward produced eccentric pocket-sized publications, full of route advice, literary information and gnomic wisdom ('a rambler made is a man improved'). Ward believed that the duties of a walk leader were to proceed with the route whether wet or fine, bring tea, provide information about local landmarks and – crucially – to see that a song was sung. But his humour belied serious intent. Their footsteps were also political: the Clarion Ramblers railed against private ownership and land enclosure, often due to grouse shooting, policed by gamekeepers with guns, who despised walkers. This famously culminated in a struggle for access to Kinder Scout in the 1920s and the Kinder mass trespass in 1932.

In her talk at CPRE's fiftieth anniversary in 1974 at Sheffield town hall, Ethel singled out Ward for special thanks and praise:

> He knew our moors and hills perhaps as no one else. Ward had a side he might not even acknowledge, an almost poetical love of the solitude and grandeur of nature.

No mere aside can do Bert Ward justice. He was a driving force behind Ethel's inaugural meeting at Endcliffe Vale in 1924, and they were unlikely allies, on the issue of the national parks and others. A photo of him in later life shows him defiant behind a microphone on a windswept hillside, trousers tucked in socks, white hair wind-tousled, one hand flung proudly in the air. In 1945, the South Yorkshire rambling community raised enough money to buy and present Ward with the summit of Lose Hill. He then gave it to the National Trust.

In the pamphlet produced by CPRE in 1944, the concept of what a national park should be was clarified by describing what it was not:

> First let the term be stripped of two unfortunate connotations – that of the National Park of North America, a huge area in which large tracts are devoted to the preservation of wild life, and that of the Municipal Park, where nature is tamed and formalised to meet the needs of the bath-chair and the perambulator.

Instead, this national park promised, 'a large tract of rural land, having at its heart an area of wild scenic beauty. In England such areas, being few, are rightly coming to be considered as of national rather than local concern.'

Ethel would note in her 1954 lantern talk reflecting on the work of CPRE that she was never fond of the term 'national park':

> One alternative suggested was 'Rural Reserves' – which I personally prefer – but it was decided that the term National Parks was so far established in the public mind and its meaning generally understood that there would be more loss than gain in making the change.

A modern audience might find 'rural reserves' equally problematic, its echoes of reservations in North America, where indigenous populations were confined after colonisation by white settlers. There's also the connotation of English 'reserve', a holding back, a sense of propriety and decorum.

The authors of the 1944 pamphlet further explained that, 'land within the boundary of a National Park would neither be one vast holiday park, nor an area preserved as in a museum. In general, it would be a tract in which rural life is encouraged and alien influences are discouraged.' We might balk today at the unqualified phrase 'alien influences', its connotations of othering: the word perhaps contains the ghost of alienation, and anything privileging the 'native' can smack of nationalist rhetoric. Lest this seems like contemporary semantic quibbling, it's worth bearing in mind the problematic legacy of 'nature writing' in Germany and how many still connect some of its polemical language to the Nazi Party. While it seems an unlikely fit – a paradoxical political belief – given their destructive and evil actions, part of the Nazis' platform included an idealised version of the German landscape and its importance in building a national community. Appealing to the more conservative sectors of the German public, environmental ideology helped the Nazis gain support as they utilised the notion of the *Volk*, the mythological ideas about the German people and their land. Evidently, this is a thousand miles away from the spirit within which Ethel and her contemporaries would have been using language like 'alien influences', but it can be helpful to reflect on why such language can be problematic in its nationalist connotations, its emphasis on 'purity' and preservation. The use of that phrase here, of course, would have been to denote the unnatural, the kinds of developments and environmental alterations which CPRE (rightly) believed were threatening an area of unusual natural beauty and interfering with the right of all people to access equally.

For some, however, there was an implicit emphasis on the 'right kind of people' (for which we can read 'people with our sensibilities'). Phil Barnes,

CPRE photographer, wrote to G.H.B. Ward in 1930 to express his reservations, the fear that a national park with road access would lead to the Snake Pass filling with 'charabancs' and tourists:

> I'm afraid I care for Kinder so much that I am perhaps taking a rather selfish view but, frankly, I would rather stay away from the hills myself and leave them to the tender mercies of the shooter and keeper, than see the delicate beauty of these cloughs vulgarised by picnic parties, as for instance the Conksbury Bridge end of the Lathkill, or the Thorpe end of the Dove, are today.

There's an echo here of the accusations of 'vulgarity' levelled at certain housing developments and new buildings in the plans for the green belt and the guidance on Peak District housing. An issue of implied taste: land to be used for certain purposes and not others. How can such moral distinctions about use be fairly drawn? Barnes admits his own partiality. Perhaps we are all guilty of wanting to preserve our favourite places for ourselves, to walk through them untroubled by the presence of others.

In 1938, Ethel wrote to the joint secretary of the CPRE Standing Committee on National Parks (one H.G. Griffin) to politely test the waters before she devoted any more of her time to the cause: 'Will you please advise me whether there is a reasonable chance of anything definite being done … ?' she wondered. 'Are there grounds for thinking that a National Park in the Peak is a possibility in the next ten years?'

Receiving no reply from Griffin, who was absent with stress, she decided to press on anyway, even if her work might come to nothing. When she did hear from him and he was pessimistic, suggesting that a national park scheme was unlikely to be a priority, she invited him to join her at a meeting in an Edale hotel, along with John Dower from the Standing Committee on National Parks and representatives of local CPRE branches and other amenity organisations.

The chair of the meeting, Professor Forster, opened by stating that a national park was not merely intended as a playground for townspeople. John Dower's response to this was measured. He emphasised that the national parks campaign was founded on a combination of three main principles: landscape preservation, access and open-air recreation, and the protection of wildlife. One aspect could not be prioritised over the others. Indeed, one aspect could not be stifled by the others.

Throughout all the early discussions of a national park for the Peak District, there was a complication: Dovedale wanted to have its own national park, separate from the Derbyshire application. Ethel was tactful in trying to persuade F.A. Holmes, chief promoter of the scheme. She wrote to him in 1942, subtly hinting that a combined bid might be more likely to succeed than several smaller ones, for 'I have been given to understand that small areas alone are not what is required.' She introduced a note of caution:

> It appears to me – though I write in deference to your longer experience – that if we work apart, we may both damage or even ruin our respective aspirations.

That deference is typical of Ethel's style, her cautious way of proceeding. Though she was strident and indefatigable when she needed to be, she was also sensitive to the egos of men in positions of power. Holmes, however, was having none of her charm on this occasion. He replied: 'We stand and fall by the Dovedale scheme. THE NATION WILL SEE TO THAT.'

Eventually, Ethel would become so exasperated with the Dovedale bid that she would say in a letter to D.M. Matheson, the secretary of the National Trust: 'I'm almost in the mood to scream at the word Dovedale!'

The National Trust supported the idea of one Peak District national park, encompassing Dovedale:

> It is not the business of the National Trust to select what should be National Parks, but it seems to it that, if a National Park is set up in the Midlands, it would be much better to have one National Park which would include not only the wild moorlands between Sheffield, Huddersfield and Manchester, but also the country in and around Dovedale and the Manifold Valley, and other parts of the beautiful country which lies roughly within the area between Huddersfield, Sheffield, Derby, Ashbourne and Manchester.

In 1945, Ethel was appointed by the new Labour government to serve on the Hobhouse Committee for national parks. This followed the publication of the Dower Report in April that year. John Dower was an architect from Ilkley and he had an instrumental role in the fight for national parks. At the outset of the war, Dower had been keen to enlist, but his health soon failed him, and he was declared unfit for active service late in 1940. By March 1941, he had joined the Ministry of Works where Sir John Reith – of BBC fame – was leading a group of talented experts in looking forward to Britain's post-war reconstruction. Dower's report argued that the establishment of national parks was long overdue. He also attempted to define what national park land should be, with a slightly different emphasis from the materials earlier produced by CPRE:

> First and obviously, the concern of National Parks must be broadly confined to relatively wild country ... mountains and moors with the associated farm lands of their valleys and fringes, of heaths, of rocky or infertile coastlines, and of the rougher parts of numerous downs, hills and forests ...

He observed that the choice of areas to designate as national parks would be 'no easy matter', and that the decisive selection and precise delineation of the areas to become national parks should follow and not precede the determination of national parks policy, 'at least in its essential features and prospective scale of operations'.

By the time the Hobhouse Report was published in 1947, an area of 572 square miles in the Peak District (including Dovedale!) was one of the four national parks put forward in the first round of designations. The parks would be governed by a central authority, but each would also have its own planning board. Even as this report was being circulated, opposition to a Peak District national park was materialising and being expressed in the correspondence columns of the *High Peak News*. It seemed that this opposition came mainly from 'mineral interests' – those who were worried it would interfere with their ability to quarry – and from farmers worried about trespass and vandalism on their land. One particular opponent called for a meeting in Bakewell to gather resistance, but Ethel persuaded him to wait until after the publication of the Hobhouse Report.

The National Parks Bill was published in 1948 and a National Parks and Access to the Countryside Act passed with royal assent in December 1949. The following year, Sir Patrick Duff, chairman of the National Parks Commission, sent the Voluntary Joint Committee in Derbyshire a draft map of the proposed Peak District National Park's boundaries for feedback within the month. This was a mark of respect for Ethel and her work: the statutory obligation was only to consult with local authorities, but Duff wanted Ethel's input at this crucial, early stage. Ethel and Gerald did raise some objections and asked for the inclusion of more areas, and they took a representative of

Ethel with John Dower (middle) on Hobhouse Committee business.

the National Parks Commission to inspect them. No changes were made, however, and they were forced to withdraw their suggestions at an inquiry in Buxton in 1951 after being advised that it would cause delay in the Peak District's designation as a national park.

The Peak District National Park became a 'reality' (strange to describe a construct thus) in April 1951. Duff gave Ethel and Gerald advance notice of this, in view of what he called their 'long and manful fight'. A 'manful' fight largely steered by one remarkable woman.

Melvyn Jones's *Protecting the Beautiful Frame* contains a wonderful black and white photograph of members of the Hobhouse Committee on a site survey visit during the national parks' planning process. Ethel sits next to John Dower on a slope, both of them with their feet crossed, holding cups in their right hands (Ethel's hand is gloved, Dower's is not). They gaze wistfully off to the left, the view that preoccupied them hidden from us. They are wearing long socks and long coats, smart clothes underneath. Ethel sports an excellent hat.

Even after the Peak District's official designation, the subject of national parks was a source of lively debate. An article appeared in *The Listener* on 21 August 1952 by Mr Brunsdon Yapp entitled 'Nature and the National Parks'. In it, Yapp debated the idea of preserving 'beauty' and challenged the Romantic view of 'unspoiled' landscapes, arguing that:

our present attitude (to nature) is not very ancient and we may well suspect that it is neither final nor perfect ... It seems that, in general, it was not until there was a class that was both leisured and educated that beauty became something that was written about and assessed in comparative terms, and such a class did not exist until the eighteenth century.

With knowledge of how landscapes are in ecological flux and how our attitudes to them may be in flux too, 'we ought not to be romantic about the hills. Their present appearance is in large part an accident ... and there is no reason for thinking that it is perfect.'

Yapp pointed out that two of the main 'threats' to the beauty of the mountains are generally said to be the damming of lakes for power or drinking water, and the activities of the Forestry Commission. This, he felt, seemed odd in a country where much of the characteristic appearance is due to the existence of natural expanses of standing water – how could the making of bigger lakes, or new lakes, be considered uniformly bad?

His opinion piece goes further when discussing transport, taking a stance opposite to that taken in publications like *The Threat to the Peak*:

> A railway up Skiddaw, or a factory at the head of Derwentwater, would certainly not increase their beauty, but even these ought not, on that ground, to be condemned outright. We have enough mountains to make access to some of them easy ... there is no evidence that the power of appreciating beauty is exclusively correlated with physical prowess. ... The same applies to motor roads; too many of them would destroy the beauty to which they give access, so let us have them few but good.

It is interesting to consider this argument in an age where we are reconfiguring assumptions around what Yapp called 'physical prowess' and access to wild places. 'Eco-crip' theories bridge disability studies and environmentalism, challenging assumptions about landscape preservation that may ignore people with access needs. In her article 'Risking Bodies in the Wild: The "Corporeal Unconscious" of American Adventure Culture', Sarah Jaquette Ray exposes the relationship between environmentalism and ableism, arguing that disability is the category of 'otherness' against which both environmentalism and adventure have been shaped and revises environmental thought to include all kinds of bodies. In the UK, poet, author and wild swimmer Polly Atkin illustrates the challenge of making national parks accessible to all bodies in her memoir *Some of Us Just Fall*, which recounts her experience of living with hypermobile Ehlers-Danlos syndrome, the difficulty of diagnosing chronic illness and her constant urge to explore the Lake District; she touches on access issues taken for granted by those living without disabilities.

Yapp's argument in his 1952 *Listener* article is framed as pragmatic more than inclusive, however. In a summary section titled 'The Real Threats to Beauty', he concluded stridently that:

> reasonable economic use of the natural potentialities of the hills, whether for wood or water, need not conflict with the development of National Parks and may indeed lead to an increase in their beauty, as the planting of the eighteenth century undoubtedly did. The threat seems to come rather from those who would sterilise the mountains from any sort of change other than degeneration.

He argued that nature does not stand still and that blanket attempts to preserve the status quo might end in 'the disappearance of that which one wants to preserve'. Gerald Haythornthwaite was very dismissive of it, calling it 'Yapp's yapp', and wrote to Pauline Dower to express his dismay that 'not long after this article was published the author was appointed to the National Parks Commission'.

In a letter to J.N. Martin of the Peak Park Planning Board, Gerald said of Yapp:

> As he does not in the least regret the railway up Snowdon I suspect that he is deficient of the normal senses which makes this abomination so repulsive to the normal eye, nose and ears.

He also observed:

> His conclusion that the appearance of the whole of the Lake District is in a large part an accident or so far as it is natural it is not going to remain the same for long, does not follow from his very brief sketch of two very small valley localities. The vastly preponderating part of the Lake District has arrived at its present form from what I think is called the efflux of time.

Another voice of dissent appeared in the *Derbyshire Advertiser* on 15 May 1952, asking whether a Peak Park planning board was really necessary. The objection here seems to have been primarily bureaucratic:

> The proposals approved by the Peak Park Planning Board at Bakewell this week are wholly laudable ... but do we need a special and pompous authority to do it? The Peak Planning Board is largely anyhow under the control of Derbyshire County Council, who could surely have managed all this without donning new clothes. Presumably the idea of the National Park sprung from the same brain that decided a rat-catcher should in future be known as a rodent operative.

Gerald immediately wrote to Patrick Monkhouse at the *Manchester Guardian* and arranged for letters to be sent to the offending publication, and friends and colleagues rallied round to correct the mistakes in the editorial (the planning board was not under the control of Derbyshire County Council) and to defend the importance of the board.

Despite the naysayers, there are countless examples in the correspondence of the Peak District National Park designation helping to guide the demarcation of other national parks. On 11 February 1954, Sir Patrick Duff wrote to Gerald to outline objections from farmers about the designation of the Exmoor and Yorkshire national parks (including trespass and damage, sheep stealing). Duff noted:

> I remember, at the North York Moors Inquiry, you offered some very interesting testimony as to the effects on farmers generally in the Peak District after that had been made a National Park. You can see the sort of ammunition which would help me in resisting the objections of the Yorkshire dales farmers: I wonder if you would be able to provide me with any ... as an ounce of practice is worth a ton of theory?

In 2022, Natural England estimated that people from black, Asian and minority ethnic backgrounds are only one per cent of visitors to national parks in the UK, despite making up about fourteen per cent of the general population. Pooja Kishinani, campaigner at the RSPB, and Ruth Bradshaw, policy and research manager at Campaign for National Parks, argued strongly that this is connected to national parks governance, where:

> Much more needs to be done to achieve diverse boards. According to the Glover Review, in 2019, 32 per cent of authority board members were female, 0.8 per cent were from black, Asian or ethnic minorities and the average age was 64. National parks are for everyone but, despite the recent small steps forward, their boards still do not reflect this.

Maxwell A. Ayamba from the Sheffield Environmental Movement (SEM) wrote on a blog for the Campaign for National Parks:

> To understand the issue of why not enough BME people visit the countryside is very complex. There's lots of discussion as to whether this is an economic issue or not, but to many, this is far more deeply rooted. It is argued that the countryside is open to everybody and so it is left to BME people to choose whether they visit or not. But there's a lot more to it than that – there's a lot of history involved – with visiting the countryside traditionally seen as a rich, white activity.

I'm thinking of Mancunian author Anita Sethi's journey of resistance and persistence in her memoir *I Belong Here*. Anita was on a journey through northern England when she became the victim of a race-hate crime. In the horrific aftermath of the attack, the Pennines called to Anita with a magnetic force: although a racist had told her to leave, she felt drawn to further immerse herself in the area she regards as her home, so she went on a walking journey, a way of saying that this is her land too. I'm also thinking of Jason Allen-Paisant's poem 'Daffodils (Speculation on Future Blackness)' in his debut collection *Thinking With Trees* where he responds to Wordsworth's famous, canonised poem 'I Wandered Lonely as a Cloud', challenging the reader to think of it differently. The piece ends with the lines:

> *Well you must*
> *Try to imagine daffodils*
> *in the black hands of a black family*
> *on a black walk*
> *in spring*

Ethel addressing a 1930s Ramblers' rally for access in Winnats Pass.

'We were taught Wordsworth's poem in school,' Allen-Paisant reflected in an interview with *Big Issue North*. 'And even I, a black person, couldn't imagine a black family wandering lonely as a cloud, or looking at daffodils!' He intended his book as an 'intervention' in the field of nature writing.

Ethel's work needs to continue: the Peak District National Park should be for everyone, and it is not 'national' if it is a playground only for certain sections of the population, if large numbers of people who live in the UK are underrepresented among its users. This work is multifaceted, but representation is surely important (in governance, in publicity, in film and literature) alongside the work of organisations like Peak District Mosaic.

In 2022, I went back to Mam Tor to retrace the route of the national park's anniversary walk. This time, Alfie walked the entire way from Castleton to Mam Tor summit by himself. We stopped at the top to eat our sandwiches and watch paragliders swoop with unlikely grace over our heads and cast shadows down over the hikers. A confused Weimaraner barked at them. As I pointed out the landmarks to Alfie from the trig point, I murmured a thank you to Ethel and to the Hobhouse Committee for their foresight, for opening up much more than just this vista.

Dear Ethel,

Why is there no statue of you in our city? There are monuments to industrialists and poets: Ebenezer Elliott holds his stony court in Weston Park, airily surveying the University of Sheffield students as they bustle or crawl to lectures. There are even (would you believe it!) statues of women: Queen Victoria casting her solemn presence over Endcliffe Park; the solid, lovely presence of the buffer girls by the town hall, a tribute to women of steel. But where are you? I imagine you bronzed by the railway station, your bird-like, alert posture, your chin angled slightly as if you're looking up to read the poem on the side of the Hallam building, Andrew Motion's much-quoted lines:

O travellers from somewhere else to here
Rising from Sheffield Station and Sheaf Square
To wander through the labyrinths of air...

We've been pulling monuments down across the country. A contested awakening. In Bristol in summer 2020, a statue of the slaver Edward Colston was toppled and thrown into the sea. There is a mounting sense that tradition does not justify itself, that we should interrogate what we celebrate through public art and place names and buildings. But where are all the new statues? Where are the black women and the forgotten revolutionaries and the old ladies? Where are you, Ethel?

I would like a Pete McKee mural of Ethel Haythornthwaite, in riotous colour, on the walls of Fargate. Cartoon Ethel, happy in the hills, smart in tweed. Your half-amused expression. I would like you to be holding a notebook in one hand and a compass in the other.

Do I find myself questioning the idea of beauty? We talk about the aesthetic appeal of wild places as if there is universal agreement about what 'beauty' and 'wild' mean. Like beauty, wilderness is in the eye of the beholder. And my picturesque may not be yours. I remember being shocked when I told a fellow writer I was moving to the Lake District in 2016 and he described mountains as 'oppressive'. I could not imagine anyone seeing the hills and not feeling liberated by them, exhilarated by the very idea of height. Before mountains were places of encounter, they were distant, savage and grand. I keep thinking of that strange line of yours in *The Threat to the Peak*:

> A thing of beauty like a grand piano becomes an atrocity in a meadow.

I wonder if beauty has anything to do with morality. Is a beautiful landscape one which is marked as little as possible by human passage? Or is it the place that gives the most pleasure to the most people? Whose beauty is it anyway? Is a mountain beautiful if there is no one there to look at it? If there is no one left full stop?

Beauty as instruction. Beauty as guide. Where to, Ethel?

Yours in productive confusion –
Helen

Ethel on her pony Bracken in the High Peak.

Peace and Amber Light

O heart that bursts with joy, that bursts with pain –
Across the hills I feel the breath of Spring.
(*The Pride of the Peak*)

In 1954, in one of her persuasive public talks, Ethel described a moment of utter calm:

> I remember as a child, one summer evening, gazing at a hawk poised in the stillness of the Ladybower Gorge, where now the buses roar over the concrete viaduct. The walls of the Winnats, towering in silence, seemed the temple of an enchanted age.

She reflected on the change to that childhood scene:

> Since then, with the increase of mechanisation, the ease of transport, the decay of the arts – perhaps the dimming of all spiritual life – huge ravages have daunted the pride of the Peak.

It is interesting how she picks up on the key role of the arts in preserving what she considered good and righteous. Ethel was a writer: not just of persuasive letters, but of literature, and her engagement with Derbyshire and its hills and moorland, its valleys, rivers, edges and woodland, was imaginative, artistic, expressed through metaphor and sound patterns and rhyme. There is a connection in her work between creativity and empathy – empathy for other people but also for animals and landscape, the character of a swathe of land. To make change, we must be capable of imagining.

Then, of course, that vision must be matched with the mundane struggle, with putting in hours of sheer effort, sheer dogged will. In the same talk, she also describes the 'slow, strenuous toil, day after day, year after year: the fierce fights, the grand victories, the grievous disappointments' of her work with CPRE:

You would be surprised at the number of nice people who come to me, smile kindly in my face and say, 'O Mrs Haythornthwaite, whenever I see a horrible atrocity in the countryside, I immediately think of you.'

Ethel resigned from her secretaryship in July 1980, aged eighty-six. She had worked in the role for over fifty years. Gerald took over as secretary and Ethel accepted the title of founder and patron. As Melvyn Jones observes, the term 'honorary secretary' hardly does justice to her contribution to CPRE and its achievements:

> Without formal training, within a context at the outset in which countryside campaigning and conservation were the exception rather than the rule ... when regional, rural and urban planning as we know them today were in their infancy, she appeared, aged thirty, fully equipped for the immense job that lay before her.

Though she had major advantages derived from her background – the financial resources available to her and the influence and contacts gained through her family – her success in pushing through significant campaigns owed as much to facets of her personality, her determination and her diplomatic skills. She succeeded because she was tactical, quick-thinking, patient, intelligent and persuasive. She succeeded because she was diligent, principled and committed to communicating with the people around her, the public she sought to convince.

Above all, Ethel would not have achieved what she did without a genuine and deeply held, deeply felt love for the environment which she had grown up around; the landscape which had saved her at her lowest ebb as a young widow, 'earth's high beauties' and how they held her sane. She believed in natural beauty as restorative. She was, perhaps, one of the first strident advocates for the connection between spending time outdoors and improved mental health. It was, quite simply, a matter of life or death for her.

Ethel's health deteriorated in her later years and she suffered from dementia. It is a heartbreaking, cruel, whittling disease, and anyone who has had their life touched by it knows the alienation and confusion it can cause, for the sufferer and for their loved ones. It is terrifying to forget, and terrifying to be forgotten. But not everything is lost. I hope that what remained for Ethel as the disease progressed were her early memories of walking over the moors, testing herself against the wind, riding miles around the boundary of Derbyshire on the back of Bracken. She had her beloved Gerald and her sister Gertie with her until the last, stalwart supporters through her life and work.

Ethel Haythornthwaite died on 11 April 1986. She was ninety-two years old. She had created a Peak District national park and a permanent Sheffield green belt through her tireless advocacy. She did not work alone, but those conservation milestones would not have happened without her. She left behind an astonishing legacy, through the Sheffield branch of CPRE which continues to fight to preserve the 'golden frame', but also through her elegiac and haunting poetry, *The Pride of the Peak*, its rapture and its precision, its invitation to travel, to imagine otherness, to climb into each new morning, keep climbing, relentlessly without fear.

I have in my hand Ethel's copy of *Across the Derbyshire Moors*, a guide to walks in the Peak District with little maps folded into the pages. At the end of a chapter on 'Whiteley Wood to "The Surprise"', there are annotations in familiar handwriting. The walk in question culminates near the 'fine, rugged hill scenery' at Burbage Bridge, 'a vast expanse of height from "The Surprise" and a sweet woodland near the end of the journey that in some places would be described as a "fairy glen"'. The author of the book asks simply: 'can anyone be such a gourmand for scenery as to wish for more?'

The delicate pencil strokes underneath are hard to make out, but I think they say something about a pair of birds: 'small, darker on the back than the belly, thin strips of white on their tails visible when flying. They sat together for a time near Eyam Moor and then took off.' From her letters and notes, this looks very much like Ethel's handwriting. A pair, separated and making their way separately through clear skies, exchanging calls. A woman, setting out to walk alone, always in conversation with her lost love. Remembering her walks with him, looking steadfastly towards the future, beyond the war, beyond the rumbling fears of the age, holding on to the constancy of rock, moss under her fingernails, weather changing her face imperceptibly.

Landscape as a constant. As partner. Language as a moor. This is Ethel's world and she welcomed us into it.

Edale, August 2023

Dear Ethel,

I am sitting here trying to finish this book under the bemused gaze of Kinder Scout, on a grey-washed day in Edale, part of me longing to be on the plateau, part of me unwilling to finish typing and close the screen. They say a poem is never finished, only abandoned. True of every piece of writing perhaps: every article, every book, every letter. Perhaps it's even true of every single half-formed thought. I am not ready to abandon this address to you. But I sit here, historically immersed, guided (as so often in our one-sided acquaintance) by the question: *what would Ethel do?*

I love the lantern talk where you enthuse about this part of Derbyshire. I can almost hear the delight and mischief in your voice. You describe realising, after some time as secretary of CPRE, that you had never crossed Kinder Scout alone in the mist. What oversight! What scandal! So you set your alarm clock early every day until the perfect misty conditions arrived. The build-up must have been intense: disappointment when the morning broke clear, the relief when you finally woke to cotton-wool skies:

> I took the early morning train to Edale. When I arrived, there might have been no Kinderscout at all, nor Mam Tor, nor Lords Seat ... I scrambled up to the source of the Noe, holding on to rocks and grass. It was so dense I hardly knew when I reached the top, save for the shadowy form of Noe Stool – like an elongated mushroom. Then I headed over the groughs to the centre of the plateau and examined my compass for the next move. When, lo, a miracle happened; the dense atmosphere lifted and in less than five minutes the sun shone, and high above me was the blue sky. I walked the rest of the day singing for joy.

I relish your irrepressible delight. I relish the way you shunned the easy route. And I relish your accuracy: on the typed script for your draft speech someone (presumably you?) has crossed out the word 'five' in the line 'less than five minutes' and replaced it with 'ten'. I imagine you sitting at your desk with the light flooding in, tapping a pencil end against your cheek thoughtfully and wondering: *five minutes? Was it really so?* Applaudable pedantry, correction of the self. You are thinking of how time operates differently in the hills, how minutes become honeyed, flowing into hours. You are reflecting on the emotional weather of the restless walker. You settle on ten. Yes, that's more like it.

Ethel, last night my son and I walked out from our campsite and followed the signs past the Old Nag's Head towards Grindsbrook. We were in our flip-flops (you would be horrified – mine were pink with a marble design). We only intended to stroll, but it was unnaturally mild and sunny for 7 p.m. and the flagged path drew us upwards. We set out towards Ringing Roger. I remembered running the same buried path, years ago, in snowfall, a day much like the one when you deliberately set out into obscurity. My son was looking for zombies to fight. He cried out, calling the crushed blackberries on the path 'zombie blood'. His motivations were as unnatural as you could imagine. And yet there we were, always striking out for the next gate, the next stone or marker. Just around that bend. We were high up before we knew it, breathless, in our unsuitable footwear. We were delighted. I was grateful to you.

In the time it has taken me to write this, the murk has lifted and Edale has begun sunning itself. There is only one imperative now. Upwards. Onwards. I know you won't mind.

Yours eternally,
Helen

A portrait of Ethel and Gerald taken for the Sheffield press in the 1970s. © PictureSheffield.com

Key Sources and Further Reading

Allen-Paisant, Jason, *Thinking With Trees* (Carcanet Press, 2021).

Atkin, Polly, *Some of Us Just Fall: On Nature and Not Getting Better* (Sceptre, 2023).

Ayamba, Maxwell A., 'Making our National Parks more diverse', *Campaign for National Parks* [website]. <https://www.cnp.org.uk/blog/making-our-national-parks-more-diverse>

Bassett Gallimore, Ethel, *The Pride of the Peak* (Jonathan Cape, 1926).

Clark, Heather, *Red Comet: The Short Life and Blazing Art of Sylvia Plath* (Vintage, 2022).

Donne, John, *Collected Poetry* (Penguin, 2012).

Harrison, M. John, *Wish I Was Here: An Anti-Memoir* (Serpent's Tail, 2023).

Jones, Melvyn, *Protecting the Beautiful Frame: A History of the Sheffield, Peak District and South Yorkshire Branch of the Council for the Protection of Rural England* (Hallamshire Publications, 2001).

Kelly, Matthew, *The Women Who Saved the English Countryside* (Yale University Press, 2022).

Kishinani, Pooja and Bradshaw, Ruth, 'We need much more nature expertise and diversity in the running of our national parks', *Green Alliance Blog* [website], (8 August 2022). <https://greenallianceblog.org.uk/2022/08/08/we-need-much-more-nature-expertise-and-diversity-in-the-running-of-our-national-parks>

Lee, Hermione, *Virginia Woolf* (Vintage, 1997).

MacCaig, Norman, *The Poems of Norman MacCaig*, ed. Ewen McCaig (Polygon, 2009).

Mortice, Zach, 'Sun, Soil, Spirit: The Architecture of Mario Botta', *AIArchitect* [website], (9 May 2008). <https://info.aia.org/aiarchitect/thisweek08/0509/0509d_botta.htm>

Paterson, Don, *Rain* (Faber & Faber, 2011).

Price, David, *Sheffield Troublemakers: Rebels and Radicals in Sheffield History* (Phillimore & Co Ltd, 2011).

The Threat to the Peak, ed. Ethel Bassett Gallimore (CPRE, 1931).

Wordsworth, William, *Selected Poems* (Penguin, 2004).

Acknowledgements

My warmest thanks to the following people for their support, expertise and guidance. The book would not have been possible without you: Andy Tickle, Moira Hunter, Tomo Thompson, Jean Smart, Gemma Thorpe, Matthew Kelly, John Coefield, Jon Barton, Jane Beagley, Don Paterson, Jess Edwards, all the staff at Sheffield Archives (especially Tim Knebel), Caroline Bolton, the trustees of CPRE, and Andy and Janet Mort.

CPRE Peak District and South Yorkshire are grateful to the many people that assisted in the evolution of this unique centenary project. Our greatest thanks must of course go to Helen Mort for her unwavering enthusiasm and dedication to unearthing Ethel's story and telling it in such a remarkable way. We also thank Fiona Reynolds, our president, for her early support for the project and for writing her insightful foreword. In the formative stages of the project, we were helped by Ed Douglas, Oliver Hilliam, Gillian Darley, and Jon and Adrian at Little Toller. We also thank Margaret Gray for her timely donation of rare CPRE ephemera.

As acknowledged elsewhere, Ethel's biography was made possible by a generous legacy from the late David Wilson. As a conservationist, bibliophile and a cousin of Ethel who latterly documented the Ward/Irons family tree, he would have been proud to help enable the book's publication.

II
The Pride of the Peak

By Ethel Bassett Gallimore

Ethel's long-form poem *The Pride of the Peak* was published by Jonathan Cape (these days an imprint of Penguin Random House) in 1926. Dedicated to the people of Sheffield, it is a hymn to the variety and splendour of the Peak District, a whirlwind, heartfelt tour through the landscape that meant so much to Ethel. Her rhymes are exuberant. Her knowledge of the places she describes is unquestionable. It brims with joy.

It is reproduced here in its entirety with only few and minor corrections to the original text. A number of these corrections were made by Ethel herself on the handwritten manuscript and a copy of the book.

To
THE PEOPLE OF SHEFFIELD
"AND DERBY HILLS THAT ARE SO FREE."

PROLOGUE

Now unto Thee, O Maker of the mountains,
Now unto Thee, O Moulder of the moors,
Graver of vales and springhead of the fountains,
My life in praise and penitence outpours:
Knowing too well its record blotched and barred
By scarlet sin, and faint with lamps unlit,
Knowing its fire for Thee yet burns so hard
My years are fervent with the force of it.

For Thou didst cradle me in nature's gladness;
I gazed into the Kingdom of Thy skies,
The colour of the flowers was morning madness
Bedecking all the grass, and my first cries
Would feign the homely cawing of the rooks:
I sang to trees, I knelt before the moon;
Deeper than from the font of fairy books
I drank of earth, and love, that fell so soon.

Then Thou didst smite with such o'erwhelming sorrow
My years arose a black and starless wall,
And begged to cease before each loathed morrow
Upon their hungriness again should fall.
And after this Thou struckst my body low
With hideous jangled nerves and ceaseless pain
From nature all unfilled and grieving slow,
That only earth's high beauties held me sane.

How I do worship Thy tremendous passion,
Nothing from Thee but flooded comes with life;
Feebly beneath Thy joy I 'gan re-fashion
My olden ferth now sterner from the strife:
Gradual 'mid the greenery 'gan to hope,
Slowly within the sunshine 'gan to smile,
And painfully beside the crags to cope
With blasting blows, and face the heavy mile.

Who can withstand the challenge of Thy vigour?
The sunlight flashing o'er the windy peak,
The summer's drought, the winter's bitter rigour,
The rains that thrash the earth, the gales that shriek?
How I do love the welter of the weather,
The veil of storm, the slanting balls that beat
Across the cheek with joy and pain together –
My God, how I do love Thy stinging sleet!

Forgive me I was e'er too wild to hery
In churches dim, although I humble came;
My grief too violent, my mirth too merry,
Is it Thy will I should this spirit tame?
O surely I am Thine, by lover's right,
Love of Thy works, I would Thy garments hold;
O Lord, embrace me with Thy stars of night,
O Christ, reject me not from out Thy fold.

Thou knowest that to drink the fresh'ning river
To me is sacrament as surely done
As tasting wine from Him, the holy Giver;
As clear a revelation as Thy Son
To me is earth; and from Thy deeps of blue
I take the comfort Thou wilt not bereave
For ever; by the Spring I find Thee true,
And by one Autumn leaf I would believe.

I am so confident of Thy compassion,
I am so proud of all Thy puissance,
I am so blessed by Thy loving passion,
I am so sure that nothing falls by chance.
By the stern spheric laws I know Thee Duty,
By air and fire that Thou wilt not destroy;
I know Thee by Thy fruits that Thou art Beauty,
I know the aim of everything is joy.

Not only this, O Light behind the lightness
No man has seen, but only caught the beams,
I know this earth the earnest of that Brightness
That none has even figured yet in dreams.
This frigid fringe of life, this beauteous rand
Unto the rest is dark as dungeon bars,
Through which we break to splendour when we stand
Nearer the essence that begot the stars.

I

SPRING with her pure sweet air!
With her rathe call of birds,
With the green bud that fills,
With her heart-aching pain:
With the world new-born fair,
With lambs and the gentle herds;
Spring with her light o'er the hills,
With her tempestuous rain.

Redmires, What is this life that's stirring in my veins?
Stanage, Upper The fire of morn, the ferth to roam out-doors.
Hurst Brook, Nothing can hold me, nought my freedom reins,
by Twitchill to I am mounting like a bird unto the moors.
Win Hill O breeze that blows, O bounding of the earth,
O white way and the grass beside the way;
O lark that sings the end of Winter's dearth,
I'm glad and grave with pleasure of the day.
The packhorse path arises, till a pole
Stands high, that marked the track beneath the snow:
Behind the uplands green declining roll,
Before the mystic moors are stretched below.
I hasten to the hill among the hills,
Over the edge, until an open vale
Tames to a little lane, whose streamlet spills
O'er slippy stones, when warmer airs prevail,
And catkins fringe the hedgerow. There's a gate
Leads to a shepherd's sward beneath the height;
And here a farm in peace is situate,
And man and mate might dwell in earth's delight.
Blue is the sky o'er fir trees, brown the brake,
Charred are the heather roots, and barren, bleak
The two great shoulders: where the winds awake
I climb the whinstone crest amid the Peak.

Mother of mountains, as I gaze from here,
So close your spirits worked within my dream,
Scarce know I if these boulders bare be near,
Or if I muse far off, and they but seem.
Only I know that with adoring eyes
I watched you young, before I climbed above,
And you are more than words from out the wise,
More to my life than friends, nigh more than love.

Moor upon moor lies round, and fold o'er fold;
Westward a ridge divides the South from North,
Limestone from grit, where sudden sleet a-cold
Strikes slant, and then the sun comes laughing forth.
O, a gay ridge, where one must run and leap
Down benty slopes and up the two high ends,
And crawl through little holes in walls for sheep;
And westward yet the bare green land ascends:

And therefrom winds a river. On the South
Sweet pastured highlands lift above their dales,
Where one may drop as in the verdant mouth
Of summer when her leaf the heart regales.
Then eastward sweeps the eye, where edge on edge
Heads the great lines of moors and whets the mind;
And dull and dark the heath now, yet a pledge
The colour ere the fall shall make men blind.

Northward I turn. The dim high plateau lands
Rise up in flights of mystery and storm
That dulls them ever; save when startled bands
Of bracken like the savage pelt and warm
Of some exotic beast are crossed by gleams:
Hope that is huge and hungering looks here.
But let us down where overrun the streams
Their banks, and westward in the early year.

Win Hill –
West, South,
East and North

The Derwent,
the Noe and
The Peak's Hole
Water

Green are the ways by the river,
                Wide and green;
There one may saunter ever
                When woodlands yean;
Where it does quietly wander,
With a shallow, sweet meander,
And curled roots tremble under
                The water's sheen.

Rivel the fruits of the hollin,
                The ash-keys dry;
Scented the air with the pollen
                That floats from high.
Silver and gold is the sallow,
The plough has rumpled the fallow,
Slow the young bullocks bellow
                Over the sty.

Coltsfoot prinks in the meadow,
                Open and bright;
Celandine hides in the shadow
                Of leafy light.
Cries to the kye the cowherd,
Calls to his dog the shepherd,
And the throstle vies with the blackbird
                Close on the night.

Clearer the stream is, and barer,
                Higher the ground;
Lower the trees are and rarer
                And pasture around.
Through the flowers and the grasses,
To the feet of the hills it passes,
Round the feet of the lads and the lasses –
                And underground.

Castleton

O, if you could but see, who have not seen,
That little limestone town aside the hills
All covered with a short turf richly green,
Where white spurs jut and strange enchantment fills
The heart delighting, then as strange a dread;
For all the land around is hollowness,
And through the hollows earn the folk their bread,
By rare blue veins in arches cavernous.
They say that at his rising o'er the town,
Such gay abandonment has here the light,
The sun at Easter dances up and down
Upon the hills, while in the caves is night.
A giant entrance cliff, hung all with green,
Stands sheer above the smoking roofs, and there
Within its vasty cavern mouth are seen
Pale men in silence weaving an old ware
From immemorial right, while jackdaws squawk
Above and round the vault. A castle high
Stands on the scarpment edge, and o'er the walk
Damp drips on fern roots and dog's mercury.
And toward the darkness of this devil's hole
Quaint little alleys play among the sides
Of houses sweating damp; and wives unroll
Crude coloured carpets, whilst the river glides
Limpid along the walls, i' the cleansing sun;
Yea, issues from the bottom of the mount,
And ten hours in the cavern's depth has run
Before it bubbles out a joyous fount.

The Peak Cavern Come you here at the fore-end,
After a high hill thaw,
Waters down from the moor-end
Flow with a heavy roar.
The darkling tide o' the dungeon's full in flood,
Swirling around to potholes in the roof,
Leaving the walls with slime and banks of mud,
And the white foam, high a-tremble, as a proof.

Enter the dark ways after,
Crouch by the candle light;
Stand and gaze on the rafter,
Vaulty chambers of night.
The river is going gently, black and clear,
Going to beds beneath, and then again
Unseen with loud and rushing noise 'tis near
Th' eternally dripping house of Roger Rain.

Wherefore is this high hollow,
Lost in its spirals steep?
Why this tremendous swallow
Plunging into the deep?
Wherefore these galleries and rooms above?
What is the meaning of the Mind that shocks
Our sight with more for wonder, more for love,
Peering within the grooves and holes of rocks?

Where is surpassed in rareness
Sheets of the stalactite?
Where is excelled in fairness
Fossils of encrinite;
Or where the shapely arches o'er this stream
Springing amid the heights three miles away?
Yet we return as from some sombre dream
Into th' ethereal whiteness of the day.

There are three passes rising from this town *The Winnats*
Of magic joy within the hills confined,
The greatest and most awful by renown
The Winnats, or the Gateways of the Wind.
Steeply the old way climbs, and at each side
Huge walls of green ascend whose limestone tops
The turrets seem of giants that have died,
So fair and savage that the heart nigh stops.
And in the place most huge and fair of all
A coign of cliff makes half the pass unseen,
And here the towering silence does appal,
And here the very air inwalled is green.
In this dread beauty, in remoter days,
Two lovers riding secret to be wed
Were murdered lone by four that knew the ways,
And near a ruined farm were flung the dead:
And straying through the forest of the Peak
Were horses found, with saddles cleared of gold;
And yet one saddle hangs for them that seek
Old tales of savagery and rumours rolled.
And strange it is that here as I looked up
On the unearthly craigs, the craig most high,
As brooding ownerful upon this cup,
Grew live in form, and like a ghoul gone by;
Some ghoul of evil long from earth expelled,
Square headed, massy shouldered, lost and grim:
With old and heathen fear my eyes were held,
Nor could I draw my gaze entranced from him.
Then high a shepherd crossed, and reconciled
I turned toward the passes' open head,
Where by a farm I saw a ruddy child,
A farm of grey, all stone and well bestead
Lee of the winds, that here to prove its name
Hurl to the hollow of the dale, and prone
Have swept men lifeless that a-sudden came
Up to these hurrying skies of billows blown,

Up to this world, all bounding, bright and free,
Where the Ridge leaps in strength, and Mam Tor stands
A fort among the hills, and scarce a tree
Crouches upon the green and rolling lands.

※

Eldon Hill and   Now the eyes wander, now the will shakes free,
Eldon Hole   Now the pulse races, now there's room for breath;
And like a loose-reined steed the strength should be,
And there is grass unhindered underneath.
Around the hill of Eldon it is gay,
It is impossible to stay the feet;
It is a wild and laughing April day,
With a great wind over Eldon and the Beet.

Singing amid the wind the larks arise,
Suspend and fall upon the earth below,
Close by an outland cattle pond that lies
Where yellow pansies 'gainst the blue sky blow.
And frighted peewits wheel above the nest
And shriek and dive, while ever here and there,
Almost as voices that may never rest
Are the strange cries of the curlews in the air.

Strange is the land, with olden mines of lead,
And network of stone fences for the sheep;
Where cattle take the belland and lie dead,
And a dread chasm, yawning, dark and deep,
Opens within the hillside; where the light
Is flashing sheets of gladness, and the squalls
Come with the zeal of youth, and driving white
With a rattle of cool rain against the walls.

Barren of walls is Eldon top, and bare
Unto the blasts of heaven, with a mound
Of bones of ancient fighters buried there,
And o'er the base the ancient roads go round.
And all the welkin's sun and storm, and earth
Goes up in smoke and heaven downward hails;
But like the shafts from God's great joy and mirth
Are the white rays over Buxton and the dales.

Under the hill a village nests,   *Peak Forest*
Peaceful under the hill;
Upon the green the sunlight rests,
It is so fair and still.
In the middle is a pond,
With a feathery wood beyond;
And the pigeons play o'er the place remote,
And the pynots chatter o'er Pedlicote.

Within the fields the young lambs play,
A black lamb 'mong the white,
They skip and sleep the mellow day,
They stay out all the night.
And from the well the healthy folk
Carry the pails upon a yoke,
And the evening lingers o'er broad Bee Low,
And the morning hastens o'er Oxen Low.

Warmer the days are growing now,
Swiftly the trees grow green,
Over the hills' uplifted brow
May is coming queen.
Lusty is the oak buds' growth,
Only the velvet ash is loath;
And the violets blow in the Conies Dale,
And the primrose opens in Perry Dale.

Dam Dale, Hey Dale, Peter Dale, Monks Dale and Chee Dale

Yea, she is here; upon the limestone heights
A dove grey haziness is seen at morn,
And brings remembered shining dear delights,
Then radiant again the world is born.
O May, why come you thus in three short days?
You we have waited bud by bud so long;
With such a burst of green upon the sprays,
With such a joyful consonance of song:
With such a gleam of flowers in the grass
Catching the light and sending back the light;
Too much it is for us whose mirth must pass,
Who yet demand for ever our delight.
And all is like two lovers, young on earth,
Who will not wait, but rush to the embrace,
And ere their joy is full the fruit has birth,
And they are growing grave of form and face.
Yet needs we must be gay this hour, and now,
Scarce hollowed in a green and sunny slope,
A shallow infant dale begins to bow,
Enticing, bare and of a dancing hope;
And swiftly dips into the dell beneath,
Hey Dale by name, that has a stripling wood
Of beeches, shedding fast the tawny sheath;
And down beyond the creamy kye are stood
With sweeping tails and shaking, angry heads;
For now the dales are broader, deeper grown,
And pasture fills the dry old river beds,
And straight and high the verdured cliffs of stone.
Until the banks are hills each side, and thick
The busky undergrowth, and still the air,
And scent and sight of flowers coming quick,
And lo, the place is very warm and fair.
With rocky lenches spread with daisies white,
And wild anemones that star the steep,
With companies of cowslips 'neath the height,
And bluebells springing lush within the deep:

And by the weedy stream the kingcups glow,
And here to consummate the vernal round
The voice of cuckoos loud the high rocks throw
Echoing through the dale a glorious sound.
Then down and down, until the last of dells
Enters the dale athwart all low and wide,
Wherethrough the surfy river sings and swells
With cliffs and tow'ring forest walls beside;
Whose leaflets glitter o'er the glitt'ring flow,
And all is raptured by the water's note,
And all a dazzling paradise aglow
With sunlight where the water crowfoot float.
And ramping butterburr o'erruns the banks,
And blue forget-me-not in heav'nly mist,
And dripping moss depends from narrow planks
In brilliance by the bubbling waters kist.
And where the river takes a horseshoe bend
It laps around a sheer and shining tor,
And in the crannies yellow foalfoot hend,
And saplings green, while yews grow darkly o'er.
And like a fairy castle in the sun
It stands, and one might ever happy be
Listening to the bees till days are done
And birds and singing in the vale of Chee.

There is a dale all green and deep	*Deep Dale,*
Which yet the hobs and pixies keep,	*Batham Gate,*
Dancing in ancient pagan round,	*the high Mosses*
Rushing the dell with a trampling sound;	
Where once a miner in the night	
Found and lost a lagging sprite;	
For the ways go up and the ways go down	
All on the road to Buxton town.	

There is a roadway high and straight,
The Romans built it, Batham Gate;
Along the line of the sky it goes
Whereon the Spring wind beats and blows:
Over the plain and over the rough,
Over the hills from the Roman Brough;
For the ways go up and the ways go down
All on the road to Buxton town.

There are in Buxton healing springs
Where ladies come, and dukes and kings,
To bathe in wells both warm and cold,
And ever the air is keen and bold
From off the wastes upon the west,
The great high wastes; and it is best
To take the wastes and not come down
Into the ways of Buxton town.

Goyt's Moss, the Cat and Fiddle, Dane Bower Hollow, near Drystone Edge, to Axe Edge

Come climb, come wander, come and view a thing
More vast, unclenchable than aught before;
Come, let us spend these last full days of Spring
'Mid golden bilberry and moss and moor;
Where nothing fills the world but white of sky
And tufted hummocks of the peaty grass,
And distant hills that dark, o'erlapping lie,
And denes to far off sunlit vales a pass.

But in the morning over these high mosses
Warm Spring to windy Spring turns swift again,
And scud on scud along the great lift crosses,
And heath and lift are one with drenching rain.
And here a wonder have I seen, a cloud,
Blocking one half of all the stormy heaven,
Come over Cheeks Hill downward, dull and bowed,
Come like a swelling smoke and nearer driven.

And yet the sun is growing great in power,
And blesses with his rays the balmy dene,
Yea, now he knows that soon will come his hour,
And through the dead brown bracken curls the green.
And in the russet hollow's warm caress
A dancing beck o'erleaps the stones and shines
Like an oasis in a wilderness,
While warm from down below comes scent of pines,

But not for long, not long; the heights once more
Whistle with wind, and hurried hailstones spin
Over the olive-coloured endless floor,
Over the bleak road to the lonely inn.
And here the denes work shallow through the peat
With loosened banks of black and sodden stuff,
And all one side a wall of blinding sleet
Batters the face with stinging kisses bluff:

And lifts anew; and far o'er gleaming plains
A rack hangs rugged from th' uncertain sky;
Earth's bosom waits for beat of rays or rains:
Then slowly mounts a trustful lark on high.
And sudden in the clear is Shuttlings Low
Thrusting his rugged wedge aloof in air,
And all the wastes with burnished colours glow,
And vales in golden afternoon are fair.

Adown the deep'ning valley of the Dane
Are rudest homesteads; chick and calf and colt
Feed on the small and sunny greens made plain,
And they are washing sheep high up at Holt.
And fair and wildly does this stream-bed wend
Within the dark and secret ways of moors,
And Gradbach Hill o'ershades its lower end,
And Gradbach meadows line its lower shores.

But bear we still along the barren sides
Up to the last and longest height of all,
Axe Edge, that all the peaty streams divides;
And we may walk these wastes without a wall,
Or ought but sheep to show that men are near,
And gritstone heads of shafts, deserted, done;
In bog and wind and wild, for ever here,
Unclaimed, unaltered, in the evening sun.

O watershed of Dane and Goyt and Wye,
O heart of vastness in the vastness old,
O southern peaks that strangely stick the sky,
Infinite view, O Head of Manifold;
Will not the cotton grass be blowing soon,
Like snow upon the thirsty land above?
Is not the summer coming; is not June
Now hazy o'er the faint green hills of Dove?

II

SUMMER with full green leaves,
With her glad fields of ease,
And when the heat is done
With her late lovers' hours.
Summer with scented eves,
And starry nights of peace,
Summer with vehement sun,
Summer with all her flowers.

Come sun and bathe me, over the stream of Dove,   *Dove Head*
Shine with thy yellow light straight in my eyes,
Make brown and red my body, even move
To warmth and mirth the heart that underlies.
O, how I love this river! Sure is none
More blissful, beautiful in all the world,
Where babbling wavelets ever gladsome run,
And ferns and summer flowers are unfurled.
Were I a cuckoo o'er the vale of Dove
I'd fly from dawn until the daylight's wane,
Calling from end to end of sun and love,
And calling, turn and fly all back again.

High and bleak the head is, 'neath a farm   *Axe Edge End,*
Within the barren, endless mountain side,   *Washgate and*
Where on a flag the beams unbroken warm,   *Hollins*
Th' initials of two fishermen are tied.
Yet even here are kingcups growing round
This purest spring that seems a sacred well,
Then steeply dips and guggles underground
And foaming reappears within a dell;
Where florets peer into its baby face,
Blue milkwort, rattle and the lousewort red,

And down the dene it happy drives apace
Till little crofts are out of sight o'erhead:
But footpaths faintly crossing mark them nigh,
And rough the banks with thorns and briars frayed,
And rougher yet and steeper and more high
With ridges that the straying sheep have made.
Until all sudden deep within the cleft
A white and tiny house, a bridge of stone
Lie, as the seal of olden beauty left
At Washgate, in the silent peace alone.
And here a comely woman and her man,
And here a boy and girl with sunny hair
Live happy as but homely peasants can,
And they will bid you in and treat you fair.
And afterward the bushy banks give way
Unto a wider, gentler slope and green,
Where fringed with trees the streamlet wends astray,
And dimly far meandering is seen
Out in the open valley; even now
The dingle strikes the limestone basin broad,
A circle green and light with pastures low,
And all around a strange exalted horde
Of mountains, some that level-topped and high
Have holdings at their feet, while two green pikes,
Doors to an outward dale, thrust up to sky,
Serrated crests that close in savage spikes.

At the high waters of the Dove, Croom Hill and Parkhouse

Shall one tread this haven?
(Cranesbill o'er the ground
Is blue by water-aven,
The great green peaks lie round)
Ev'n at the high end of the heavenly stream,
So beauteous, so aloof, sublime, unfound;
And step as in some pure and lofty dream,
And bare the feet, for this is holy ground?

From the fields I wonder
These small booths and rough
Should stand so peaceful under
The awful limestone bluff;
Here seems too rare a place for men to dwell.
And yet I stay and never have enough
Of grass and stream and hills and flowers' smell,
And roses on the walls of Hollinsclough.

I have dared the terror
Of the devil's room,
Through which the world of error
Well nigh had 'scaped its doom;
For here the lost one tried to hang him high,
And high among this beauty yet does loom
The snake in Eden; in the mount awry
With evil and with good, O magic Croom.

Orchids paint the meadows,
Purple spotted, white;
There is no taint of shadows
On all the meadows bright,
On all the plains the buttercups make gold.
Let us then drown all sorrow with delight,
Let us forget the world with wrong is old,
Let us lie down within the fields of light.

And yet the wanderer, who goes　　　　　　　　*The hills above*
In valleys only, never knows　　　　　　　　　*the dales*
The full breath that our land exhales –
The great hills over the dales.
O the sunlight never still,
O the wind in Summer chill
O'er Aldery Cliff and Hitter Hill
Over the great High Wheeldon.

The great dale walls are flat above,
The great flats look out o'er the Dove;
A thousand kine are batt'ning there,
And goodly 'tis to fare
Miles and miles and no man meet,
While the plantains knock the feet,
And breath of the kine is floating sweet
Under the great High Wheeldon.

This is the pith of life, to go
O'er Carder Low and Waggon Low,
Over the tumulus on high,
The lands that live in the sky:
Over Pilsbury Castles old,
Over beet on beet untold,
And head upon headland skyward rolled,
Over the great High Wheeldon.

Glutton Mill,   Broadly the dale makes on, and long and straight,
by Pilsbury to   Lined with the level hills, its mighty sides,
Hartington   These ancient hills of pasture, amply great;
And o'er the base the waxing river glides
Wand'ring, and the base is swamped with light,
With gold of buttercups and green of grass;
And sun is warm on timid calves, and white
The hawthorn in the little lanes that pass
To every humble homestead's muddy yard,
To every whitewashed homestead and remote
That has a rough and jealous dog on guard,
Under-the-hill and far off Crowdecote.
Here in the happy meads the river shines,
With light through ragged robin on its brink,
And wantonly in lazy loops entwines
The narrow necks of sward one would not think
Could from a shorter course the current stay;
Until at length the foot-road mounts a hill,
And with some show of strength the stream makes way
Toward the ivied wall of Ludwell Mill.

And in the widening plain are houses seen,
And with a widening sway the waters run,
And where a path descends the hill from Shene
Flow with a broad sweep into Hartington.

☙

Into this ancient market town   *Hartington*
A hundred farms their milk send down,
Left at the lonely turns in cans,
And trundled in with carts and vans:
And cheese is vended, green and good,
That more than twenty weeks has stood;
And everything from the rise of the sun
Comes in and out of Hartington.

Here is a white and open square,
And here is held the Summer fair,
Cattle are brought and cattle sold,
And many secret fortunes told;
And when the whiteness casts its heat
The boys play cricket in the street,
And linger late and call and run
Till ten strikes out at Hartington.

Cattle go lowing through at light,
And back they lowing come at night,
While to the pond within the square
The ducks at morn are driven there;
The ducks at eve are driven out
With stick and stone and boyish shout;
And everything till the set of the sun
Goes in and out of Hartington.

☙

Beresford Dale,   And now some hundred paces from the town
Wolfscote Dale,   There stand, in all the leaf of summer dressed,
Milldale and   Those dales that give the river Dove renown,
Dovedale   Flowing within the limestone gorge compressed.
Beyond a field, 'twixt little mound and mound,
The cliffs converge, o'erhung with branches green;
Then might one ask if this be earthly ground,
Or if some haunt forbidden to be seen.
Sheer rise the rocks above the narrow bend;
The stream is still, the foliage stirring not;
Down from the rocks the long green mosses pend,
Campion riots; this the sacred spot
Beloved of fishers and revering men;
And by the Pike outstanding in the pool
Of deep green water, where 'tis seen again
Beneath in mirrored loveliness, the fool
All blust'ring with the world's last busy nought,
Might hushed be to a moment's wonderment
And worship in this verdure, to a thought
Of how such beauty reigned, and what it meant.
And then all changes, and aloof and bare
A small enchanted valley opens wide,
Where lies concealed the wolf-abandoned lair;
The banks fall back, with screes on either side
And thorns; a little wind the water whips,
That like a silver riband gleams alight;
And back the mind to fairy legend slips;
For this is just that place of dread delight
Encountered in the stories of the world,
Whereto a maiden comes with knight on guard,
And stones from jutting scars on them are hurled,
Or bands of lawless foemen press them hard.
Then brighter shines the sun, again the trees
Gladden the banks, the stream is gold with glee,
And by the reeds and dragon-flies and bees
Down the rejoicing dale runs merrily;

Until the banktops closing out the sky
Become a somewhat sombre awful wall,
And where toward the final dale they nigh,
Halt at a turn before the best of all...
The white rocks tapering spire, the hillsides tower,
Moonpennies bleach the cliffs and gorse above
Glows like an orange flame; high Nature's power
Condenses radiant at the holes of Dove.
The glancing water's wide and daunts the eyes,
Or rushes narrow through the shady rocks;
The dale is pressed with trees and sunlight lies
On every brilliant leaf, the blackbird mocks
At dulness; all the glades are filled with bowers
Of birds that warble amorous rhapsodies,
And in a warm entranced bliss the hours
Shine on, as though this timeless Heaven is.
O dale of Dove, the last green gorge of light
Is made alone for man's encrownèd days,
When life at its most glad and reckless height
Two lovers move delirious in these ways,
Naked with riotous claspings unrestrained:
Or an aged woman, having lost her mate,
Walks here with tears of joy that soon regained
Shall be his arms, and their old happy state.
Great is the heat now down the dale, and wide
Green stretches by the shallow reaches trend,
And there are leppings to the other side,
And we are drawing nigh the lower end.
And mimulus is here and meadow-sweet,
And on the banks the willow-herb is high,
And scent of earth and nettles rife the heat
Brings forth, and all the scents of hot July;
And out beyond are folded meadows seen
Ripening to the summer's rich reward,
Ample and glad and green and gold between
The two green mountains that the entrance guard.

Thorpe Cloud and Bunster	But lo, a stifling dulness through the heat Pervades, and black above the Hill of Sin A storm is beating, and aloud and fleet Filling the dale like steam comes deaf'ning in. There is a rumble far, and then a flare, Then flash on flash, and rattling roar on roar Pass and resound within the portals bare, And with great drenching tears the heavens pour: Till in huge burning network up the sky The forkèd lightnings show and show again, And bluey sheets of æther wide and high Light up the gloom amid the streaming rain. And for an hour we gaze in silent awe; Then with a few slow drips the torrents cease, And all the sunlit fields and valleys o'er, And o'er the entrance of the dale is peace.

Well-dressing	There is an ancient custom in the dales The while the place is pigmented with flowers, The while the short and sunny clime prevails, The people catch two-handed at the hours. With stitchwort pale and campions, With ragwort gold and dandelions, The folk are glad with colours and with smells, With all the blooms that blow they dress the wells. They frame the wells with mosses and with clay, And prick the blossoms in like coloured stars, All in a bright mosaic live array, In squares of blue and red and golden bars. With roses wild and serpent-weed, With cinquefoil and silver-weed, With service in the churches and with bells, With priest and holy book they bless the wells.

It is a pagan practice from the prime
As when a naiad dwelt in every spring,
And may it dwell and flourish for all time
In Derby dales; for 'tis a sacred thing,
With rushes fair and rattle-bell,
With grasses and bog-asphodel,
With every leaf that grows and bud that swells,
With feasting and with dance to dress the wells.

※

Now in the morning let us mount away *Up from the dales,*
To where the white walls and the white roads go *by Arbor Low and*
Over the green and callow hills, and pray *Over Haddon to*
Up in the lonely fane of Arbor Low. *Haddon*
Time tells us not why these flat monster stones
Lie in a solemn silent circle high,
Within a wall of earth, nor whose the bones
Beneath the barrows near the blowing sky:
Only that men lived here and drew the breath
Of wind with heathen health, and knew the sun
At every point of day, and life and death
With earth and hills and stars were strongly run.
O what a buoyant day it is, around
The blue is crossed by swelling billows white;
Behind there is the leaping pasture ground,
Before there are the scented meadows bright.
Indeed it is a breezy, swinging land
With many green and weathered burial mounds,
With hallowed rings of trees, and farms that stand
By groves; this happy time the tedder sounds
Tossing the hay, and there are wains of hay
And ricks about the outline of the sky,
And haycocks which th' exalted meads display
(Their acres gored with dales) and we on high
Bear on, o'er every crazy tumbling wall;
Above the ancient cupelows of lime,
Up where the oats are growing green and tall,

And where the sunny slopes are sweet with thyme.
Until the fields descend and down we tread
Where still the lants and furrows old are seen,
And one side all the sorrel's blowing red,
And one side all the grass is blowing green.
And we are hard upon the valley where
With golden light and verdure over all,
As growing in the very greenwood there
Stands like a house of magic, Haddon Hall.

Haddon Raised on a rugged scarpment of the wood,
And fashioned to its feature, tower on tower,
Court upon court, terrace on terrace stood,
Is this fine trophy of man's building power.
Let us who mar with masonry the land
In humbleness 'fore ancient Haddon stand.

Because to build, it is a godlike art,
Like forming of the vales and barren stones,
And like the nests of birds should be a part
Of earth, the offspring of her flesh and bones;
And here is the essential harmony,
The strength of rock, the balance of a tree.

O what a multitude of turrets fair,
Like to a crowded city in a wall!
O what a sunny cobbled inner square,
O what a darkly panelled dining hall!
O what a beautiful long gallery
With windows o'er the terrace lawns to see!

The terrace lawns are laid upon the steep,
And buttressed grey with bastions of lime,
For pleasaunce and for holiday to keep
All in the green and singing summer time;

And here the fleckered light of sun comes through
Upon the sward, between the leaves of yew.

It stands above the shallow, shining stream
Spanned by a carriage bridge with arches three,
As beauteous as a palace in a dream,
A home, a paragon of symmetry.
And one might even say in gazing there,
That man has made the very earth more fair.

O, in a hot and sunny day   *Manners Wood,*
Let us cast all care away,   *Calton Hill,*
Let us be all blythe and gay   *Calton Lees*
And go to the Calton pastures.
Up the wood behind the hall,
Up the road with the grassy wall,
Up to the beeches growing tall
On top of the Calton pastures.

The great grey boles they stand upright,
The glittering tips are out of sight,
The grove is flooded full of light
And peace on the Calton pastures.
And all day long the beeches ring,
With chaffinches that loudly sing,
As singing were the only thing
To praise the Calton pastures.

Up beyond a hill-slope green
Yet another hill is seen,
A farm in the little dale between
Beneath the Calton pastures.
Hill and dale are fair with fun,
Down into the dale we run;
Wild apples yellow in the sun
At foot of the Calton pastures.

The Chatsworth Valley

Let us go over to the lordly vale,
That lies with lordly Summer in its breast;
Let us with feasting on the lawns regale,
And underneath the mighty branches rest;
In this the time of steady summer heat,
When all the fields their plenteous offspring hold,
In August when the hay is pilèd sweet,
In August when the corn is turning gold.

Yea, let us taste of meat and drink of wine,
And waxen well with sun throughout the day,
And gaze along the valley's wide decline,
And up the wooded hilltops far away;
And all the hot hours watch the cattle stand
With still reflection in the ample stream,
And see the deer go bounding o'er the land
That in the twilight airy phantoms seem.

Low in this land of Beulah at one end
There is an inn of stone and builded fair,
Whose fronts toward the dusty highway tend,
But on the back side lies a garden there;
A level green of peace with flaunting flowers,
Where once a peacock walked upon the lawn,
Where men stay bowling in the evening hours
And looking o'er the valley and its corn.

And every time that corn again is high
It seems to me more goodly than the last;
I gaze on wheat and barley, oats and rye,
And never blows a field I can go past.
I list the different sounds the breezes make
Over the golden, bended, speary host,
The wheat that rattles and the oats that shake,
And never know I which I love the most.

O shady Derwent, sunny Baslow bridge,
With niches white the river jutting o'er;
O fields of Bubnell 'neath the Froggatt ridge
That seemed in childish dreaming days of yore
The quintessence of Summer's art to please,
With the hot limewhite road by Calver Mill,
And the cool Hassop road beneath the trees,
So in my years of ripening seem they still.

And when I stand among the corn or hay
In all the goodly warmth and goodly smell,
Where the young men with sunburnt faces sway
At work, primordially I crave to dwell
Under the open season's endless round
For ever with my love in golden mirth,
In union with the sun and with the ground
Blessed by the overmastering joy of earth.

And when I wait amid the summer night,
And drink the pure and sacred scent of flowers,
So poignant with the peace of rich delight
That earth to heaven through transcendental hours
Transpires; when light is late upon the hill
And in the lonely cot the lamp is red,
I sigh for all earth's heart, and to fulfil
Immortal hunger here unanswerèd.

Lift up, my eyes, then to the edge of stones
Above the valley, cloven, dark and strong,
And let me climb up by the naked bones
Of this bold land, and nigh her outlines long.
There is that makes the mind a mightier thing
And opens wide the free and venturous doors;
High up above the windy Froggatt ring,
Paling to purple splendour, lie the moors.

III

AUTUMN with dew that lies
Betimes; and when 'tis sped
Air genial over all
Wafting, then frosty kist.
Autumn with windy skies,
With colours brown and red,
With her extravagant fall;
Autumn with baffling mist.

The coming of the heather

Like unto dawn along the level heights
Is the first pallor when the buds put forth,
Like unto faint light out of darkest nights
O'er all the moorlands cast and to the north:
So pale the stranger here might ponder; 'Lo,
They seem, the swarthy sweeps, like heather dead.'
But we, who've waited all the year, we know
With quickened breath, has come the promisèd.

Slowly the pale white turns to purple pale,
And turn the twigs to warm and mossy green;
The tight buds feather into flowers frail
Beside the brilliant leaves of bilberry seen.
And O, th' exquisite fairness of one spray
Backed by the open season's sky of blue,
With the bright leaves minute set all one way
Against that strange inexplicable hue.

A few days more, and then a sort of bloom
Comes on the moors, as on the fruits of wine;
A warmer tincture, tempering their gloom,
That they are purple we can now define.
And clusters of a warmer colour still
Kindle the heart; the gorcock quiet lie,

That soon will beaten fly from hill to hill,
While bracken green above the head is high.

Then reigns indeed the purple, growing rich;
We deemed we knew the colour, but so rare
It flows o'er airy edge and hidden sitch,
Dumbfound we gape: nought ever blew so fair.
And as for me, a numbness takes my life,
Numbness for ought save heather, but for this
Exhilarated fervour, fiery strife
For the free purity of heather's bliss.

And more and more, a floor of purple pile,
And multi-purples filling sense and soul;
Too good, too beautiful, for mile on mile
Over the balmy heavenly moorlands roll:
Till as to stun the very reason fast
And flood the flowing feelings overfed,
Like flame from heart of fire there glows at last
Out of the marvellous purple, marvellous red.

And so amazing is the coloured earth
The eyes are dazzled with unwonted strain,
There comes a new and fierce exalted dearth,
And yet the sweetness surfeits unto pain.
Lapped as in waves of red the boulders lie,
I fall in heather, clasp it with my hands,
And smell the heath, and see it 'gainst the sky,
And yet on fire for more my need expands.

Ah, magic colour on the magic moors,
And paradisial sward among the flowers,
Is there in all the plains, on all the shores
An ecstasy like these few weeks of ours?
Like cloth of heaven o'er the bright hills spread,
The limbs can meet not, nor the soul its gladness;
Like feast and dance before the bridal bed,
Like unto marriage, like to music's madness!

*Longshaw
sheep-dog trials*

Glad is the old rock, Mother Cap,
On a morning of the year,
When blossoms gay her feet o'erwrap,
And dogs and shepherds near;
In bright September weather,
When folk come all together
Under the brilliant heather
Beside the Longshaw meer.

Whistles the shepherd like a bird,
The dog bounds over the green,
They tempt and steer the silly herd
The hurdle gates between.
In bright September weather,
When folk come all together
Under the brilliant heather,
And Longshaw skill is seen.

Circle the dogs around and wide,
Or stalk with a stealthy tread,
Crouch for commandment, glowing-eyed,
Fly and Moss and Jed.
In bright September weather,
When folk come all together,
Under the brilliant heather,
With blue sky overhead.

*Froggatt Edge,
Curbar Edge and
Baslow Edge*

I will go up, I will go all alone
Up to the moors, the blue and cloudy sky;
Even to those fierce rands of blackened stone
Whose ramparts sharp across the moorlands lie:
Where lies the water black and cold,
Where gleams the bracken tipped with gold,

Beside the grasses pale and by the sedge,
On high above the cliffs of Froggatt Edge.

Boldly the boulders o'er the valley stand,
And lift their heads against the lofty air;
Their jutting crags command the lower land,
Like couchant dragons looking from their lair.
And near a chasm, high and deep,
Enwalled with whinstone, swart and steep,
A tortuous stump, maniacally glad
Twists high above the rout of rochers mad.

And where the way is mossy and most fair,
And most the heath grows by the boulder wall,
Towers a windy promontory there,
The most exalted windy rock of all
And in the bracing blowing air
I mount the lenches stair by stair,
And hear the wind like waves upon the shore
Rush in the heath and in the fissures roar.

And back on the unchanging Flat of Stoke
Stand rugged stones in circle, whence the sun
The whole of day was seen, and where the stroke
Of sacrifice was at his rising done.
And out on Ramsley's brackened floor,
And high on Eyam's black barren moor,
And far o'er Offerton and all around
These olden temples stud the higher ground.

As mete it is; O hillmen here that knew
To hery in high places like to these,
Surely such instinct it was high and true;
Believing do I bow upon my knees.
Before I loved the written Word
Bare rock and sky my spirit stirred
To deism: at flooding of the day
Blindly, and like some poor dumb beast, I pray.

There is a lonely bay within the edge,
High rocks it has like huge hieratic doors,
A low rock in the centre on the ledge,
Above the heaven, below the valley floors.
Our blood is of that early brood,
Uncivilized, untamed, and crude:
I know for all the cultured vales beneath,
Here is my element and here my breath.

❧

White Edge Moor,   Wild are the moors and wild remain
Totley Moss,   That forever waste have lain,
Stoney Ridge   Under the wind and under the rain,
                          And wild blows the weather;
                          Tameless they by time or town,
                          In heather coated, turning brown,
                          With marshes waving up and down
                          And bents and bracken where there grows no heather.

Here the moors they widen out
And the heights are thrown about
Far away to Kinderscout,
    And great is the welter:
And the heavens making dole
Rain upon the fens that roll
Around the naked Wooden Pole,
    And moss and rushes where there lies no shelter.

Over the moors the roads of old,
Walled the driven herds to hold,
Roughly run and wide and bold
    And where lands are lonely.
Straight the stony Ankirk way,
From the edge of the moors to the edge of the hay,
In wind and wet the whole of the day
    Traverses where there stands one homestead only.

Dark are the olden walls each side,
Dark are the olden posts that guide,
Dark the sky and the moors beside,
And dark grows the heather.
And I reck not strife nor pain
If I may come in wind and rain,
Again, again, and yet again,
O'er moor and marish where there blows all weather.

There is a valley, open, broad, and long,   *Burbage;*
That winds with grassy road by Burbage brook,   *Carl Wark and*
Which dances with a pleasure-giving song   *Higgar Tor*
Beneath a little brig within a nook.
And here the voices of the moorcock shake,
And still the sumptuous covering is seen
Of purple heather and of golden brake
Declining with the splendour of a queen.

And all one side the water-bed a wall
Of crag uplifts, and opposite are tors,
Flat-topped, with blackened sides that steeply fall,
A buttress 'gainst the foe in far-off wars.
And where a lower bluff thus guarded lies
Three sides around, the folk of early days,
Fierce, and in fear of savage enemies,
Upon the fourth a rampart stark did raise

Of boulders now a man could never heave.
And in the glowing ripeness of the day,
Under the work these warriors did leave
We stand and marvel; till we turn away
To Higgar Tor that towers up beyond,
That still to mighty faery does belong,
For on the top there is a faery pond,
Up in the fort of rochers high and strong:

Of which the farmost swarthy heap looks o'er
A callow hollow, deep and very lone;
A rillet gushes down the hollow floor
And at the bottom is a farm of stone:
The while the whole commanding stands a tor
High in the sky with turrets either side,
Wherein a lord might live, and from the door
Look downward like an eagle in his pride.

But turn we unto Burbage once again,
And climb until the frothing beck divides,
Until the barren peaty head we gain,
And view the brackened vale and rocky sides.
And ever and again that I am here
My heart is brast, my eyes with tears are full,
And seems in all the mountains far and near
I never saw a sight so beautiful.

And all about us now is Stanage Moor,
And dim upon the skyline Stanage Pole;
The bronzing tussocks of the olive floor
In marshy flats toward the skyline roll.
And far along the waste of White Path Moss
Bog-driven boundary stakes are dimly seen,
Whereby the lost can grope a way across
The silent loneliness that lies between.

The cold comes keen upon the blasted road,
The mist lies low along the fens each side,
The dusk upon us like a god has strode
And dampness, and my soul is satisfied.
The wind blows with a loved and lonely sound
Among the row of thorn trees; from within
The eyelet of the little house that's round
A red fire glows, the days are drawing in.

Where the moorland waters flow *The seven halls*
Round the Burbage, round the Noe,
Are quiet homes of stone and low,
O the Hall of Leam!
Built by a yeoman for his sons,
With lattices and mullions,
Or by the ancient lordly ones,
The Hall of Hazlebadge.

Nigh the washy leys and low,
Looking o'er the Darrant slow,
With lawns that to the Darrant go
Lies the Hall of Nether:
And 'neath the moor upon a hill
With close, three-cornered, small and still,
With ivy o'er the window-sill,
The Hall of Hazleford.

But O, the rounded trough and stalls,
The dovecot in the garden walls,
The narrow gateway topped with balls,
Of the Hall of Highlow!
And under Robin's lonely mark
With high and stalwart entrance arc,
With barns of stone and shippons stark,
The Hall of Offerton.

And eke the lathes are built as good,
Of single trees of oaken wood,
From rig to ground the cruks are stood
O the barn of Glover!
While the air within to let
Slits and circle holes are set,
And stored and stout the walls stand yet,
The barn of Gotherage.

These are buildings that should be
Under the moors so strong and free,
A pride to own, a joy to see,
O the Hall of Eyam!
Worthy of a land so rare,
Where the lungs may breathe the air,
And the soul grow straight and fair,
O Hall of Hazelbadge!

Under Stanage Now in the gaiety of green and gold
Edge. Cowper Glows russet, and the leaves float singly down,
Stone to Crow And now the rocks and brake their banquet hold
Chin Within the mighty sweep of black and brown.
O my wide moors, what air you have, what strength
And body blows along that potent ledge,
Whereunder we will walk the whole fierce length,
Even the jaggèd, sombre Stanage Edge.
It is triumphal Autumn, with a wind
And warmth, and moors on moors their darkness lift
In lines that grow more dim and grey behind
Until they fall in scarpments high and swift.
And what palatial splendour! Near and far
The wide and folding floors are diapered
With auburn bracken pressing cliff and car,
And heath maroon and bilberry turning red:
With whortleberry green and emerald moss
And pines and yellow oaks within the cloughs,
While speeding clouds throw shadows dark across
The carpet of a hundred gorgeous stuffs.
Here a deserted quarry stands, around
Huge millstones, black, uncarted, lie about,
Like to the wheels that rumbled o'er the ground
Of giant wains, and put the hordes to rout.
And bord'ring this abandoned site of toil
A road disused, with grass-grown wagon lines,

Now travels through the peat and sanky soil
And out into the open moors of Strines.

~

These are great moors,　　　　　　　　　　　　*Broomhead,*
There are no walls upon them,　　　　　　　　*Bradfield and*
They sweep towards the north with scarce a field;　*Strines Moors*
Strongly the rain pours,
And wind goes tearing o'er them
At morning when the rainbows span and yield.

Bright the sun gleams
Through lashing of the raining
Adown the trees the banks of Ewden hold;
Copper the sunbeams,
The air of Autumn staining
From hues of red and madder, brown and gold.

Over the syke
The ancient gap defending,
The high hill gap between the south and north;
Over the Bardyke,
With streamers grey depending,
The huge lift hurries, till the sun comes forth

Warm o'er the dene
Again, where leaves are flying
And squirrels sit within the forks of pines;
Water is bright seen
Afar in valleys lying –
Agden and Damflask, Daledyke, up to Strines.

These are great moors,
There are no walls upon them,
And very swart they are and grand and old;
Brilliant the light pours

Where fiery grass waves o'er them,
At evening when the sun is sinking gold.

☙

Derwent Edge

Yea, they are very grand and very old;
Nothing is grander than the waste we climb
By Foulstone Dike toward the headline cold,
And roars the wind a roar of ages prime
Through the Raddlepit Rushes wild,
Through the Brogging Mosses siled,
O'er Derwent Edge, the fort and throne of Time.

Back on the moors it lies, in loneliness
Left as it rose from out the ancient seas,
Without a tree or beast or man to bless;
Only these rocks and this eternal breeze
Buffeting the Cartledge Stones,
Buffeting the Hurkling Stones,
And knots of stones that stand like fortresses

Bold on the black, uplifted moorland wall;
In eerie forms, in solid phantasies,
The while the clouds go scudding over all
Eastward and dull across the whitish skies.
Close to the cliff of Dovestone Head
Clustered lie the Cakes o' Bread
Round which the black and blowing water flies.

Bitter the rand, so black, so grim, so high,
So brutal blows the wind athwart the edge
That grit and gravel 'gainst our faces fly,
We cruddle, hands and knees, along the ledge,
('Neath the high Salt Cellar rock,
Under White Tor's swarthy block)
Blown into bog and slough and burnished sedge

Back from the brink: for all the other side
A plunge of air pervades, and vaster heights
Heave dimly through the void white and wide,
The High Peak that the hungry soul excites.
All his wastes before us stand,
Headed by that tableland,
Hope of the day and terror of the nights.

Farmost of all the giants on the verge
A line of boulders like a galleon
Stands ploughing ever through the heather surge,
With the loud wind behind to drive it on;
Tearing round the stony masts
With remitless roar that blasts
The lonely towers the lonely moor upon.

Mighty the moor lies stretching at their feet,
A falling vast of undulating sedge,
And heather dead and spongy moss and peat;
At times an eagle nests within the ledge.
Dreadful it is, and dark, and free;
Dying, I think my soul shall see
The Wheelstones on the line of Derwent Edge.

O wind that's blowing from the west,　　　　　　　*Beneath*
Strong and black with rains;　　　　　　　　　　*Derwent Edge*
The Autumn wind that will not rest,
But breath and sinew strains
Till every tree is wet and bare,
And leaves in train are whirled in air,
The day is jealous of her beams,
And yet they come as jewel's gleams.

Beneath the edge the streams arise,
In the clough heads brown;
They spring from black rocks near the skies,
And come through bracken down,
All steep and foaming in the groughs,
And o'er the dark and stony roughs;
Then through the sloping pasture's calms
To drive the dripping wheels of farms.

Over the edge the blackness drifts,
Under the edge the storm
A-slanting whips, the tempest lifts
The mists like flames that swarm
Within the clefts of Whinstone Tor;
The welkin swallows up the moor,
And dims the blocks upon the hill;
But 'neath at Grainfoot all is still.

And sudden o'er the waterhead
Play the rays of the sun,
Like a topaz flushed with red,
Or gold carnelian.
And filled with iridescence fleet
The rushes glizzen at our feet;
The heron rises after storm
From out the Dovestone gully warm.

Above the springs there are the wastes,
Trackless, sodden, vast;
Far overhead the tempest hastes,
And all the rain is past.
Upon the lofty banks are pines,
The sun upon the low banks shines
In radiance: it is enough,
For peace is in the Far Deep Clough.

❧

There comes the time in Autumn's latter end   *Derwent*
When she does know her mellowness o'erthrown,
Though with these tears her life she does defend,
And this loud breath that's blown the leaves all down.
One night the stars they sparkle strangely bright,
And in the early morning it is chill,
And see the meadows and the brays are white
With print of firstling frost; while o'er the hill
There is a new-come thickness in the air,
As though the year did silent yet resist:
And then the coldness conquers, everywhere
There hangs a pall of dull, cinereous mist.

❧

The heavens lighten; over the hills at morn   *Cockbridge,*
The sun is gleaming, pale and white and cold;   *Wooller Knoll,*
And lo! the snow the high ridge does adorn   *Jaggers Clough to*
Sparely, beside the inky scars, and gold   *Grindsbrook*
Resplendence very rarely tints the heights
That open now in mystic vast array;
One rising ere another sweep alights
In majesty bewild'ring far away.

Into the vasts then, up the northern side
Of massive Win, engraved with steepest groughs
Of frosted bracken, flooded streams that slide
With loosened shale and noisy to the cloughs.
And as we climb we lose the light of sun,
And watch the mighty flanks grow grey with cold;
Yet pray we all his brightness be not done,
That still the copper brake his warmth shall hold.

But no, the cold air leadens, in the cliffs
A foam of hail is frothing, high and dim;
And swift the storm about us beats and whiffs,
Far off the mountains and the hollows swim.
The storm comes bellowing from Wooller Knoll,
We cannot see, nor hear each other speak;
We strive to gain the point, and backward roll,
Until with clussomed hands and stinging cheek

We win, and reel adown the other side:
And now our object rises full in view,
Huge Kinder gluts the vision loft and wide,
His plateau scored with stream-beds sliving through
The towering cliffs that fence it all around,
And plunge his streams into the valley under,
While all his head is cloud and blackness bound;
And comes an awful sound of Winter thunder.

And Winter, can I brave you, even here,
Without the sun or warmth or verdure blest?
But rain and dark and snow and rocks and fear,
With days too swift for pause, too cold for rest.
And monstrous bulk of moorland, spreading arms
All black and toothed and belching dreadful blast,
Those very mists they cow me with alarms,
And can I pass that unseen rand at last?

O cease, faint fear and scaddle idleness,
That nothing ever risked, nor ought achieved;
Is this the mood to gain that sacredness,
That power and beauty that the mountains heaved?
For is not this my soul's love, this the sum
Of all my land, the terrible and fair?
With all the ferth that joy endows I come,
With all the strength that grief has brought, I dare.

IV

WINTER with cold close morns,
With woodlands dark and dire,
Where yet no life is lost,
But sleeping waits to grow.
Winter with long red dawns,
With eves a vault of fire;
Winter with kingly frost,
With his celestial snow.

At last, at last, O high, inexorable,   *Kinderscout*
Huge peaty plateau, come I to your feet;
With huge desire, with hope inexplicable
Those crests remote and foaming sides I greet.
Something of age-long turmoil stirs my life,
As when the crags were but God's stormy dreams,
And dreams condensed they stand, with godhead rife,
And godhead pours eternal down the streams.

Oft in the coldest stronghold of the year
I've stormed this tableland, and time again
By force of fog and snow I've come not near,
And every prize I've won was won with pain.
No place has e'er so beat me with rebuffs,
No place has e'er so crowned me with delights –
The damp and bitter scent of all its cloughs,
The trenchant darkness of its frosted nights.

Like to some kingly monster of the prime
Is Kinder, black, unwieldy, fenced and strong;
His sleepy cloughs toward the fastness climb,
And oozy ridges line his plateau long.
The mist comes hurling high o'er Edale cross,
And sheep upon the benty bastions graze,

And swiftly falls the dreadful dark across
The far ferocious rind of Fairbrook Naze.

When it is Autumn neath 'tis Winter here,
When sun is on the valleys, here is mist;
At highest noon the plateau's cold and drear,
And still as though the elements were whist.
When frost is powdering the grass below
Thick icy pillars line these walls of peat,
And when the lees are sprinkled thin with snow
Here lie the drifts in depths of many feet.

I have been lost, where dimly Kinderlow
Had set his savage spines against the sky;
And felt the rocks, yet knew no way to go,
So thick the snowy lift, the mist so nigh:
And evening neared, and whiteness turned to grey.
And 'neath the snows were boggy waters black,
And soary peat and heather hummocks lay
Around, without a point or wall or track –

And thought of those two men a Winter past
Benighted on the plateau, wandering round,
Beclammed and cold, until they fell at last,
And after days of search were frozen found.
And then a light like pale Icelandic dawn
Winnowed the wastes, and ere the day was done
Surges o'er the mass majestic and forlorn,
Celestial billows roseate in the sun.

O you are very awful, lifted floor,
And how shall one that awfulness recount?
The solitude and grandeur of a moor,
Th' infinity and glory of a mount.
Of such a drastic beauty other lands
Seem tame, with such a deadly force you pull,
Like some fierce lover with relentless hands,
Till all my soul and all my frame are full,

Full to the rim with dreadful ecstasy:
And in the darkness high I take your kiss,
Remorseless and appalling, wounding me,
Yet not one throw of angour would I miss.
And how you change! With generative joy
Begot of vigour, sunlight bathes your cloughs,
And oaks and ollers down the banks enjoy
His warmth, and bracken blazes by the groughs.

And once, in Winter sun, beside a stream
Sleeping, I Kinder saw beatified;
I drew from earth a fair exalted dream
Of what she was, or what is prophesied.
A radiance poured, more pure than ever here,
A thousand naked forms and joyful sprang
Up every clough, and on the plateau clear
They met in ring and raised their arms and sang!

Bounding the boglands of the far High Peak	*Barber Booth,*
A bow of mountains stands with one way out,	*Upper Booth, Lee*
Even the ancient track that passes bleak	*Farm and Cottage,*
And high o'er Jacob's ladder, round the Scout.	*to the Cloughs*

But leading to that blowing wilderness
The open field-path travels fair and green
Between the tors, and into its recess
Toward the holy head of hills serene.
And as it nears the entrance to the heights
A heavy sense of this o'erpowering land,
Lord of its lonely habitants, unites
With the antiquity of farms that stand
So stark and rude at bottom of the bluffs;
Till at the ending of the pastures smooth
Lies the remotest hamlet of the cloughs,
Smoking amid the stillness – Upper Booth.
And turn we now to the exalted vale,
Narrow and long, that leads to Edale Head,

Where flows the noisy Noe with banks that shale
Beneath the knolls, and deeply in its bed:
With slender birches pale that line its sides,
And hebbles for to ford the flooded stream,
Where ridges seam the shaggy mountain hides
Above, and bright is Winter's sunny gleam.
For now the days have fallen in the year
When all things long adread are come at last;
And lo the settlement is not so drear,
But like some sacrifice that's over-past
With torment of the soul and heart that's riven –
When all the happy loveliness must cease –
Knowing that everything is highly given
Austerely to the spirit comes a peace.
And midway 'twixt the valley's head and feet,
E'en in a site so far and beautiful,
It seems a dwelling-place for Heaven meet
Or childish dreams where every hope is full,
There stands beside the way a farm of stone,
And near a shippon built against the height;
And in the narrow steading low and lone
A cottage old is crowded, washen white.
And O it is the fairest place to stay
The earth affords; a rose tree o'er the wall
Pushes its happy fronds in morning play
Into the deep-set open casements small:
And in the morning too the cocks and hens
Clutter, and shaggy sheep come through the yard,
The big dog barks, and robinets and wrens
Hop on the ledge of snow that's frozen hard.
And here a little woman lives, her face
Is kind with smiles, and bright as any bird
She sings and bustles all about the place,
And tends her guests with many a pleasant word:
And ever is a cheery fire and red
To warm the parlour with its crooked floor,
And ceiling with the sturdy beam bestead,

And cupboard old with brasses on the door.
And all beneath the awful solitude
And bristling flats of Kinder, that at dark
The warmth and lamplight seem more strangely good
Of this sweet haven and enchanted ark;
Enchanted, for one never can forget
Those beetling heights and stars above the snow,
Nor yet to loose the lattice and inlet
The living night and voices of the Noe.
But come, pass on: in loneliness sublime
Rises the path, the mountains grow more steep,
And rears the head before us all the time,
An arc of rocks, and up the sides are sheep.
Until we halt before a tiny bridge
Striding the Noe at foot of all the cloughs,
At foot of all that level lofty ridge,
At foot of all the foaming, shining groughs:
And stand within a hollow, huge and green,
A socket of the hills with widening rim,
Whose crown of crags celestial is seen
Aloft upon the empyrean brim;
And Jacob's stee is by the angels trod
Of Jacob's dream, and all this water hurled
Like fountains from the living breasts of God
Into the sacred places of the world:
Sacred in beauty, where the eye in flights
With worshipping ascends, above the beds,
Above the bogs, and those majestic heights,
Lost in the heaven o'er the fountain heads.

O Winter, sometimes in these days severe,   *Kinder Low, Edale*
A day of such perfection does befall,   *Rocks, Noe Stool,*
Of such a purity, so bright, so clear,   *Crowden Towers*
That nought excels it in the seasons all.
Now such a morn of frost betides,

When snow-bones streak the dull blind-sides,
And we shall rise to the ethereal ground
That's crescented with giant merlons round.

Then nigh these 'splendent rocks that head the vale
Most surely it were paltriness to pine,
With breaths of frosty freedom to inhale
Like fiery draughts of effervescent wine;
And grand it is to scale the stones,
And tingling through the blood and bones
To feel that lively instinct sure as doom,
That we and they are of one primal womb:

One primal fountain: as we round the crest,
E'en walking like to seraphs high in air,
The host of runnels roaring down the chest
Are foaming 'neath us in the crater fair:
And far above the strongest flow
Stands the exalted stool of Noe,
And icicles they blikken down the streams
The gladness of the Everlasting dreams.

But as we near the farmost cop, a dread
Comes cold upon me; I would go no more:
A rout of black amorphous blocks is spread
As though the earth had cast them ere she bore,
And left them in prenatal hours
Laughing and grim by Crowden Towers;
And something ere the normal life was made
Commanding pulls, and I am dire afraid.

For now I know that ancient awful spell
That drew to earth the brides against their will,
Forever with the kings of earth to dwell,
And dance and dance and know not good nor ill.
I shut my eyes, I feel the rocks,
With dreadful glee my spirit mocks

At all the truth: I cower back in fear,
Knowing I must not linger lonely here.

Yet he is calling far, this fierce strong mate,   *Stony Ford,*
Calling from out his far mysterious soul;   *by Broad Clough,*
Now when the frost is rent and full in spate   *beneath Cluther*
His torrents o'er the tow'ring blackness roll.   *Rocks to Kinder*
O godlike air of Kinder, blowing wet   *Downfall*
And cold across the ledge at Stony Ford,
What an eternal sea of hills is set,
And sunlight 'yond the roof of dulness poured
Upon Mount Famine and the South Head[1] height,
Over the sodden Roych and Chinley Churn:
Yet fare we not toward those waves of light,
But hugging still the plateau walls we turn.
Turn from the distant radiance into gloom,
The monstrous mountain rand that opens wide,
And though it lead to danger or to doom
Nothing can keep me from that twofold side;
Which forking widest here with grimsel arms
Narrows unto a scarcely seen recess,
Where something white and smoking drops and swarms
As in the hidden haunt of holiness:
So far, so dim, so inaccessible,
It heaves the high and spiritual desire;
That stumbling to the blackness terrible
With no light but the yearning spirit's fire,
With no path but the sobbing spirit's hopes,
With no right but the will that's clean and strong,
Lunge we against the huge unlevel slopes
Of heather clumps and tangled bracken long;
Slowly toward that mystic place, the edge
Wrasty above, and crossing many a brook
We come at length upon a jutting ledge

---

[1] South Head, pronounced Suth'ud.

Where kneeling, o'er the wonderment we look...
Far in the junction of those sombre sides,
And sheer adown the scar five hundred feet,
Browning the black with his eternal tides
Plunges the downfall, with the sunlight fleet
Crossing his dazzling watercourse; but most
He pours in coldest shade of either wall,
In hurry ever changing, host on host
Of foaming wavy fringes hang and fall,
Or like a moving sheet of stalactites
Curtain the craggy steeps with folds anew,
All glistening white with scintillating lights;
While fore-anent the misty golden view,
Widening between the two gigantic rands,
In plateau after plateau fair extends;
The bulk of all these crude, unbondaged lands
O'erseen as from the world's remotest ends.
And even up as down the water streams,
For the strong blasts toward the gully blown
Forever lift his hair in hoary streams,
That vertical against the crags are thrown,
Up from the roaring stony base; and still
Climbing the cliffs the froth ascends like fume,
And breaking back from every rocky sill,
Till high above the topmost rim the spume
Leaps like a naked spirit in the sun;
And o'er the stream-head on the lofty plain,
Through which the calm and shallow sources run,
Descends in fall of blessèd golden rain.

The Downfall

Why do I worship here,
Torrent of the mount?
Is it thy beauty so regales my eyes?
Is it the ferth of thine exceeding fount
Startles my soul to naked, glad surprise?

Is it this lonely crevice in the heights,
This corner in th' unconquered plateau's edge?
Is it my body that the air excites,
Passionate, adoring, on this ledge?

Why am I troubled here,
Torrent of the mount?
Is it that all this kingly joy and force
Minds me of that my heart would not recount,
Lest it recall in its torrential course
All my fierce cataract of grief and glee,
Now bound within the frozen cliffs of pain?
O, only lord that ever mastered me,
When shall we meet in majesty again?

Why am I weeping here,
Torrent of the mount?
I cannot see thy form for scalding tears,
Only the dazing whiteness at thy fount;
And thine eternal roar is in mine ears.
Only thy spray falls heavy on my head
As in a radiant baptism divine;
Fountain of founts, give me whate'er bestead
A spirit pure and passionate as thine.

Why am I kneeling here,
Torrent of the mount?
Deep 'neath declining sobbing I am glad
This Force that flows will pay beyond account
With greater good than we have ever had.
I know not if 'tis sacrilege to see
This sight; with splendour grows my vision dim:
This mount is holy, and this mystery
Is poured from out the sacred Life of Him.

The Plateau

Now at the head of all this fiery foam
Stretches the mountain flat for seven miles,
And though through all the waves of peat we roam
No change the endless heaving waste beguiles.
Sometimes the plateau's broad, sometimes 'tis stret,
But nought but black and ever lifting ledge,
But black and ever falling syke is set
Till the amazing daystones front the edge.

O but the air is loft and strong and pure,
Unbreathed by man and far o'er common earth
This fortress everlasting does endure
Of mighty sky and mighty plateau's girth;
And this strange river Kinder steely bright,
Between the horrid ebon hillocks curled,
Seems with its cold and its unearthly light
The watchet water of another world.

And in this weather-breeder afternoon
We tread the trenches, fierce and full of joy,
Yet knowing that the Winter darkness soon
High over all the heaven will deploy.
And this is where the mist comes like a pall,
Knowledge is naught, and chart and compass vain,
And where the lost and roving loudly call:
The mocking murk sends back their voice again.

And wandering in these ghoulish lumps of swart,
And in these oozy ditches all the same,
Hale men like maniacs have toiled and fought
Till night or cold or weariness o'ercame.
And some were slockened in the sancomes here,
And some the roky precipices tried,
And fell. E'en now the dusk is drawing near,
And we must hasten to the farther side.

About the time the light is growing cold   *Mill Hill, down*
We come down from the plateau by the Scout,   *Ashop Clough,*
That like a dire devouring beast and bold   *near Rough Bank*
His frightful head of blackness pushes out: *to the Snake Inn*
And heaves on high, an horrid awful mound
Exultant in unmitigated power,
While from his sides the swart and swampy ground
Sweeps back within the shadow of his tower.
If shadow e'er could darken such a dye
As blacks the boggy fleets of Ashop Head,
And this huge mummock snarling at the sky;
For the wide wilderness around us spread
Seems fathoms deep in foul and porous black,
As though the world itself of black were made,
As though the primal substance were of black,
To cow the light and make all life afraid
To issue ever coloured, ever fair;
That through the lofty sources of the stream
Knee-deep amid the blackness oozing there
We plod, as in some sullen, sombre dream.
Sombre, but breeding high desire like storm –
And yet 'tis ease to dip a little down
To where the boggery grass begins to warm
The swarthy trenches with a burning crown:
And young of limb to leap adown the grifts,
From high and tufty rig to sodden soil,
Where the old blackened snow lies dead in drifts,
Or dripping in the sandy ditches coil.
And one side is the Moss of Featherbed,
And one side is the great black Ashop Moor,
The shelving brooks from either watershed
With peaty scum toward the Ashop pour;
Within[2] and Upper Red and Nether Gate,
Wafting wet wind from off the mystic vast:
And all the while the stream is growing great,
And all the while the dusk is falling fast:

---

2   Within, the name of a clough; pronounced with'in.

And all the while the Ashop's valley door
Is widening and its banks are growing high,
And dim below is seen the river floor
Beside a distant road and hostelry.
And now indeed the darkness closes round,
And now the darkling banks are broad and rough,
And from the track the slape and skerry ground
Slips deep, precipitous, aside the clough.
And we are passed unto the bleakest part
Of all the Peak, at Kinder's northern feet,
Even to its untamed and barbarous heart,
Wherein this winding, white, unsheltered street
Traverses through the wonders of the wild.
Down in the vale we turn to look aback:
Far up to Ashop Head the banks are piled
In lap on lap of black and dimmer black;
And sky is cold and valley dark as ink,
But all the leaping waters of the flood,
From burning base unto the hilly brink
Are dyed in crimson sunset like to blood.
But O, great wonder of the dark and light,
I am not worth to take this splendour in:
I turn from out of glory to the night,
The silent road and solitary inn.

The Watersheds.
Featherbed Top,
Shelf Moss

Later; upon the dire ferocity
Of river loud, and dread and canted walls,
And the far summits dimly massed on high,
The weird and ashen reign of moonlight falls.
Yet is the queen but rarely seen herself,
And with the night there grows a mistiness,
Upon the sources of the Higher Shelf
The wind beats with increasing bitterness;
And raps the hands and fills the head with pain,
And like a demon howling loud does blow;
Then something strikes the cheek more soft than rain,

And from the north there speeds a storm of snow.
The first great storm of Winter, and the last;
Thicker the flakes come, thicker is the sky,
Till all the dome of heav'n is falling fast,
And in our flesh we feel that this will lie.
The dark wastes change to grey and then to white,
And sifted through the fences low and stone,
Hour after hour throughout the silent night
The snow in pale fantastic heaps is blown:
And all the tussocks lie like mops of snow,
And benty blades as seaweed fingers are,
Across the roads the blizzards raw will blow
The drifts aslant and regular, and bar
All traffic from Old Glossop to the Snake:
The gullies fill, the tracks are blotted out,
And only show by gaunt and frozen stake
The Doctor's Gate and passage of the Scout.
And still the vasts become more featureless;
Toward the grey dawn still the feathers pour,
All over Bleaklow's monstrous dreariness,
And over cruel, stark Cold Harbour Moor;
Over the Grinah Stones and Yellow Slacks,
Over the lonely Benches of the Shelf;
And not a hare athwart the mosses tracks,
And not a fowl is heard in hollow delf.
Until with morning health the sun comes forth,
The heavens rest above their quarry bleak;
In silence, east and west and south and north,
In dazzling brightness lies the mighty Peak.

Here for a fortnight lasts the shroud of white, *North Kinder*
And tattered in the sitches lingers more,
Congealed 'neath moaning blasts amid the night,
And dwindled in the daytime by the thaw.
But in the latter days there comes a cold
That seems to seize the blood and chill the bones,

And every font and trough and drip does hold,
And lines with iron rime the fearsome stones
That fringe the front of Kinder in the shade.
For now the frigid frost a tyrant reigns,
And forms a scimitar of every blade;
While the hard snow is blown against the panes,
And pundering off the dark, forbidding edge,
Sweeps frore across the coldest face of all,
Up where the keiking crags are like a hedge
Of pikes and spears along the northern wall.

Seal Edge, Blackden   Then with zest of health, the zeal of life,
Rind, Crookstone   The strength of Winter and the force of fight,
Knoll to Edale   With the great heart rejoicing for the strife
We start to storm the last and steepest height;
Where all the huge blind side is grey with cold,
And where the snow lies late into the year,
And o'er the Seal Flats, level, long and bold,
The Seal Edge soars, a monstrous barrier.

The ice is thin upon the river low,
The ice is thick aside the steepy streams,
The frore snow swishes o'er the frozen snow,
The Seal Edge vertical, unvanquished seems.
The wind comes colder, darker grows the shade,
The torrents all are bunged with snow and mute;
Beneath the mountain, joyously afraid,
We gaze to where the lonely topstones shoot.

And up the muniment ahung with snow
We scramble slow with feet and hands and knees,
Clutching at covered tufts that loosely grow,
And slipping from the slape and hidden screes.
And straight o'erhead along the swarthy rim
There glows a line of orange, ruddy light,

Wherein the snows, wind-shifted, dance and swim
Upon th' entranced, illuminated height.

And we will not be conquered, 'tis our day,
The last great day that crowns the seasons four;
Searching the rind of rocks we find a way,
Not looking down, but ever tense before,
Hand above hand and cautious limb by limb,
Slowly unto the plateau's height we gain:
A sea of brightness surges o'er the brim –
Panting we fall upon the sunlit plain.

Ah, waving waste of wonder, yet once more,
Amazed and worshipping I see you lie;
But this time bathed in sun, a brilliant floor
'Neath the celestial beaming of the sky.
And all about the great air-giving vasts
With hollows high and headlands sweep untamed:
I pray that while the earth and beauty lasts
These lonely glories be not spoiled nor shamed.

And bearing eastward till the height of noon
We slome along the vasty burning plain,
Now toiling to the tufted crests aboon
Then plunging in the dazzling drifts again:
Until the mountains south are dimly seen,
And crossing where the springs of Jagger slope,
Coming from off the whiteness to the green
We stand in reverie 'neath the cross of Hope.

On to the green; for O, great change and fair,
All of the southern flanks have shed their snow;
A tinge of balminess imbues the air,
The icicles they swiftly melt and flow.
The hills lie radiant, the aching dreams
Press warm from out the love-awakened earth;
Instead of silence is the noise of streams,
Instead of life congealed, desire for birth.

What is this roaring in the vale below?
This turgid race of waters brown and wide?
Is this the slim, the young, the playsome Noe,
That tears away its banks on either side?
Yea, for from off the stores of every knoll,
From out the lonely clefts of every tor,
Down every rumbling clough of Kinder roll
The snows in splendid passion of the thaw.

The twilight's nearing; yet it is not cold,
And still there is a twittering of song;
O in the dawn shall come now as of old
The carols waxing louder and more long.
Far over Rushop Edge the glorious sun
Races his chariot that will vanish soon;
The planet Venus rises; day is done:
High in the heaven hangs the crescent moon.

———

Lees

And then a few days later, all alone
I walk again in that exalted vale,
The which so long the winter's grip has known,
Which now the warmer, gentler airs regale.
And wander in the evening mildly round,
Aside the benty hill behind the farm,
And watch the rabbits racing o'er the ground,
All dreamy with a new and vital charm.
And as I slowly climb there comes in view
The Clough of Crowden, russet in the rays
Of mellow sunlight, 'neath a placid blue,
And scarcely can I stir for sweet amaze.
Yet warm and glad remount, the peaty tops
Are burnished gold, the peaty pools are gold;
A rainbow shaft arises straight and stops,
Even the savage rocks the radiance hold.
And all is procreant peace and amber light;

Nothing could be more blessèd than this plain:
A shepherd's voice comes up from 'neath the height,
And downward step I to the fields again.
The horses to their shuds are moving slow,
This day the franzy kine were letten out,
And heated in the blood they snort and low
And caper in the open lees about.
And from the cottage in the early morn
Was heard a stirring in the shippon small,
A tender, weak and white-legged calf was born,
That looks with wond'ring eyes from out the stall.
And back toward the beastgate come the sheep,
But nearing slowly, for the ewes are great;
I cannot hold my senses, I must weep
For all the joy of love, for mate with mate:
For all the life that's quick'ning once again,
For all the little lambs a-gambolling,
O heart that bursts with joy, that bursts with pain –
Across the hills I feel the breath of Spring.

LOCAL WORDS

Aboon: above.
Beastgate: summer pasturage.
Beet: a field name, pasturage.
Belland: a disease, a poison from lead ore.
Blikken: to shine.
Blind side: the north side of a hill, away from the sun.
Boggery: an adjective, from bog.
Bray: a hillside.
Brig: a bridge.
Busky: bushy.
Cant: slope.
Chest: a row, series (Howden Chest).
Clam: to starve, pinch with hunger.
Clussomed: benumbed.
Cruddle: to cower, bend down.
Cruks: arched oak timbers supporting roofs.
Cupelow: cupola, a furnace.
Ferth: energy, life.
Fleets: land through which streams flow.
Fore-anent: opposite.
Fore-end: the early spring.
Franzy: wild, fresh.
Gate: a way, road.
Glizzen: to sparkle, shine.
Grifts/groughs: trenches, little narrow valleys worn by water.
Grimsel: sooty black.
Hebble: a short wooden plank over a stream.
Herd: a herdsman.
Hollin: the holly.
Keik: to stand out, project.
Kye: cows.
Lants: ridges of ground between the furrows of ploughed fields.
Lathe: a barn.
Lench: a shelf of rock.
Leppings: stepping-stones.

Leys: pasture or grass-land.
Meer: a pond.
Mummock: a heap.
Oller: alder.
Punder: to be blown or whiffed away by wind.
Pynot: a magpie.
Rand: border, margin, edge.
Rig: the ridge of a house.
Rind: ridge, bank, border.
Robinet: a robin.
Rocher: a rock.
Roky: cloudy, foggy.
Sancome: a quagmire.
Sanky: boggy, spongy.
Scaddle: timid.
Shippon: a cowhouse.
Shud: a shed.
Sitch: dyke, ditch, ravine.
Skerry: gravelly, slaty, stony.
Slape: slippery.
Slive: to cut.
Slocken: to saturate with mire, overcome.
Slome: to wander aimlessly.
Snow-bones: pieces of snow left after a snow-storm.
Soar: black mud.
Steading: a farmhouse and buildings.
Stee: a ladder.
Stret: narrow.
Sty: a stile.
Swallow: a place where a stream enters the earth and flows underground.
Syke: a ditch.
Watchet: wan, pale.
Weather-breeder: a fine, warm day in autumn or winter.
Wrasty: angry.

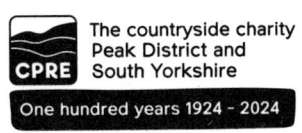

About CPRE

Peak District and South Yorkshire

CPRE Peak District and South Yorkshire is the countryside charity. We believe the countryside is for everyone, wherever they live. We want a thriving, beautiful countryside for everyone to enjoy.

We work to:
- Connect people and countryside; so that more people can enjoy the benefits of the countryside.
- Promote rural life; so that the countryside and its communities thrive.
- Empower communities; so that people can help improve and protect their local environment.
- Grow our capacity; so that our work can continue now and in the future for generations to come.

Underpinning this is our commitment to tackle the climate emergency. It sits at the heart of everything we do.

For 100 years we've worked to promote, enhance and protect the Peak District and South Yorkshire countryside. We shall continue to do so for generations to come, but only if we can secure generous support from people who are passionate about the Peak District and South Yorkshire countryside. As well as being CPRE Peak District and South Yorkshire, the charity represents the Campaign for National Parks in the Peak District National Park.

For more information and to get involved, please visit *www.cprepdsy.org.uk*